The Fords in My Past

Harold L. Brock

Society of Automotive Engineers, Inc.
Warrendale, Pa.

Library of Congress Cataloging-in-Publication Data

Brock, Harold L.
  The Fords in my past / Harold L. Brock.
    p.   cm.
  Includes index.
  ISBN 0-7680-0599-X
      1. Ford, Henry, 1863–1947. 2. Ford, Edsel, 1893–
1943. 3. Ford, Henry, 1917–1987. 4. Brock, Harold L.—
Friends and associates. 5. Automobile industry and
trade—United States—Biography. I. Title.

TL140.F6 B76 2000
338.7'6292'0922—dc21
[B]   00-026531

Copyright © 2000 Society of Automotive Engineers, Inc.
                    400 Commonwealth Drive
                    Warrendale, PA 15096-0001 U.S.A.
                    Phone: (724) 776-4841
                    Fax: (724) 776-5760
                    E-mail: publications@sae.org
                    http://www.sae.org

ISBN 0-7680-0599-X

SAE Order No. R-270

Cover photo courtesy of Norman Rockwell Family Trust.

Foreword

The mission of this book is one of sharing with the reader the "rest of the story," as Paul Harvey would say. Please allow me to share some of my personal experiences and observations from the time when I worked directly with the three Fords—Henry Ford, Edsel Ford, and Henry Ford II—as well as some of the experiences of my coworkers.

Many books about the Fords have been written by historians from cold archival material, and a few books have been written by key Ford management such as Charles Sorensen and Harry Bennett. Although some of this material has interested me, I hasten to point out that I found some of it to be self-serving. Also, much of the archival material has echoed newsworthy material reflecting bad publicity. I firmly believe that this does not portray the true character or the dedication and concern of the three Fords to create a better world for all of us. Their personal entrepreneurial spirit, their vision, and their willingness to pursue projects that offered little promise of great financial rewards should be made a matter of record.

As an octogenarian, I realize that time is running out for me. Having shared some of my early experiences with others, my many friends in the automotive industry suggested I put my recollections in print. I hope these recollections will give the readers more insight about the Fords, as perceived by one who had the privilege of working with them and observing their unusual talents.

Acknowledgments

❖

My thanks to Thomas Rockwell and the Norman Rockwell Family Trust for permitting me to use the beautiful portrait of the three Fords as a cover for this book. Norman Rockwell was a genius in capturing important people and events during his career. The Ford portrait was produced and used in the Ford Motor Company book, *Ford at Fifty—An American Story*. It was editorially produced by Picture Press, Inc., with Joseph J. Thorndike as editor.

I appreciate the photographs furnished from Robert N. Pripp's book, *Vintage Ford Tractors*, and Randy Leffingwell's book, *Ford Farm Tractors*. I would recommend these books to anyone interested in more detail about Ford tractors.

I am extremely indebted to those who trained me in the skilled trades area and engineering disciplines. My career would not have been as successful without the dedicated support of my supervisors and my many fellow workers. Credit for this book also should go to my many friends, who have encouraged me to record my exciting experiences in working with the three Fords.

Without the loving support of my family, I could not have pursued or endured the time-consuming challenges and opportunities during my work life. Their gracious acceptance of my many absences from important family occasions, because of business commitments, has been my loss. They have accepted that the elder Henry Ford instilled in me at an early age his observation that "idle hands are the hands of the devil."

Prologue

The rise of industry in America has been told through thousands of stories. As we enter a new millennium and reflect on the past century, no period of automotive history has brought more exciting developments and changes in lifestyle than the first half of the 1900s. This book spans the late 1920s through the 1950s. During this era, the automotive industry was evolving from the Ford classic Model T, which had cornered the market, to the development of many differing competitive concepts. Several unique designs for components and styling concepts occurred during that time. By the end of the 1950s, the science of design and production methods had matured, thus bringing about more commonality of concept. Therefore, body construction, chassis design, and components were no longer as unique as was typical of the early years of the century. As automobile designs became more standardized, the early entrepreneurism of Henry Ford diminished and his interests drifted to other activities.

The cloak of world renown had descended on Henry Ford long before my arrival at Ford Motor Company in the late 1920s. His vision of providing economical transportation for the masses was a matter of record. With adoption of a moving assembly line to assemble cars, factory costs plummeted. Ford wanted to pass the savings on to the consumer, but his stockholders opted for greater dividends. Thus, Ford purchased their interests and reduced the Model T roadster to a retail cost of $260. Furthermore, with unselfish motives, he increased workers' wages from $2.50 to $5.00 per day. For the first time, common laborers could afford to purchase an automobile. Henry Ford's philosophy of service to mankind, rather than focusing solely on profit, continued through my years of association with him until his death. His abhorrence of those who "shuffled paper" and his negligence to monitor financial affairs were of great concern to the Ford Motor Company management team before Henry Ford II reorganized it in 1946.

This period of the 1900s was marked by aggressive union activity and the involvement of Ford facilities to produce armament for World War II. Both events caused Henry Ford great concern. His subsequent death and the reorganization of the company marked a milestone in the future success of the Ford Motor Company.

I recently visited my early "haunts" around Dearborn, the Product Engineering Center, and Henry Ford's Fair Lane home. With great nostalgia, I leaned against a sturdy oak at Fair Lane and reflected on the time when the view was of fields of grain gently swaying in the breeze, orchards bursting with spring blossoms, and birds hustling to build nests. This pastoral scene has been replaced by a large shopping center, with Ford Motor Company corporate headquarters visible in the distance. The natural wonders that were so dear to Henry Ford no longer exist. Sadly, I remember him telling his farm manager not to plow the fields until the bob-o-links had finished nesting.

Please allow me to share with you my personal experiences of the time when working relationships were less complicated and a one-on-one management style prevailed at the Ford Motor Company.

Contents

Chapter 1

Henry Ford's Vocational– Technical Schools

Although this book is not about me, I must tell you briefly how I was fortunate in being placed in a situation that brought me into association with the Fords. This story could have been told by others of my early classmates and possibly better. However, most of my classmates have gone to greener pastures without putting their experiences with the Fords into print.

With the importance being placed on vocational and technical education today, I hope my early personal experiences may help others assess the importance of early training of this type. Such training is extremely important for those restless teenagers who need to be challenged by working with both the mind and the hands in creative activities.

Henry Ford was a visionary. In 1916, he recognized that trade and apprentice schooling was important to provide future well-qualified technicians for industry. At this time, the industry was run primarily by master-mechanic-type disciplines, with few engineering graduates. Henry Ford and his mentor, Thomas Edison, believed that the mind and the hands were the instruments of creating worthwhile things. Both men were artisans who believed that "idle hands are the hands of the devil." Similar to today, many young people of high-school age during the 1930s became restless and dropped out of school. Philosophically, teenagers are no different today than they were years ago. As with myself, many teenagers today become bored with the daily formal training by parents and teachers and by their demands that do not support the young person's biases or personal interests. The great urge of wanting to be independent and to fly before the wing feathers develop is typical at this age.

I hasten to add that I was one of those rebels. My father was an accountant at Ford Motor Company, and he wanted me to follow in his footsteps. Thus, he enrolled me in commercial courses in the public schools. Much to my dismay, I quickly discovered that my classmates were young ladies taking courses such as bookkeeping, shorthand, and typing. These subjects bored me, and as a result, I failed in all subjects. I was convinced that a future in commercial subjects fit me as well as socks would fit a rooster.

Unfortunately, at this early age I did not appreciate the many charms the young ladies were developing. Likewise, being surrounded by so many members of the opposite sex resulted in more attention than I could handle. My father recognized that I was headed for trouble, and he arranged to have me enroll in the Ford Trade and Apprentice Schools at the age of 15 in 1929.

The headmaster of the school was a warm but strict gentlemen we called "Pop Searle." The faculty consisted of educational graduates with substantial shop training. The school was based on teaching teenage boys the high-school curriculum in a formal classroom environment on a rotational basis of one week in class followed by two weeks in shop activities.

When enrolling in the school, each student took a hot shower and was examined by a doctor. Each boy was issued a heavy industrial apron and a beanie-like skullcap, both safety items to ensure that hair or clothing would not become caught in machinery. For safety reasons, jewelry such as watches or rings was not permitted. The caps and aprons made us teenagers appear as if we were serious recruits ready to face the world.

The shop classroom consisted of the 1,200-acre Ford Rouge factory, with approximately 100,000 employees. The factory was the world's largest industrial complex at that time and was located by the Rouge River. Ford Motor Company owned iron ore deposits, coal mines, and lumber mills, as well as the means of transporting materials from them to the Rouge factory. The raw materials such as iron ore and coal were brought into the factory by large boats and by rail. Coking ovens processed the coal into coke for foundry use. Benzene, the by-product of the coking process, was used for a period of time as a fuel to propel the cars. Iron ore was produced for castings. Steel was produced for forging, sheet metal bodies, and castings. The factory was vertically integrated and produced almost the total product—a complete car. The

At the Ford Trade and Apprentice Schools, students were taught both a traditional high-school curriculum and shop activities. (From the Collection of Henry Ford Museum and Greenfield Village)

Rouge factory was the first "just in time" operation of automotive manufacturing. This was accomplished by 27 miles of conveyors and 93 miles of railroad lines within the factory. From raw material to the finished product, materials were moved through this enormous facility. The final product was driven from the assembly line.

Ford Trade and Apprentice School students' work in the factory was performed with full-time workers, with the discipline that most teenagers needed. Each student was under the jurisdiction of the department foreman. At the end of two weeks of intensive shop work beside the production workers, the student was ready for the ease of classroom studies. Simultaneous formal education and shop training permitted students to observe how education applied to the real world of work. Textbooks covering the subject matter, associated with factory production, were not available; therefore, the Trade School textbooks that covered math, electrical, hydraulics, shop, and tool and die making practices were developed from actual shop applications.

As a student, I helped prepare the loose-leaf textbooks, and I worked several weeks on a slow calculator to develop mathematical tables of the natural trigonometric functions. (This monotonous chore would have been simple with the computers of today.) This personal experience made the studies seem output-oriented and of great interest to me. I felt proud to be accomplishing something of importance at a young age. At graduation from Trade and Apprentice School training, each student received a high-school diploma and an apprenticeship certificate recognizing his training in the many disciplines of the manufacturing processes. My training included drafting, tool and die making, pattern making, foundry practice, electrical maintenance, metallurgy, and engineering. At a rather young age, I became knowledgeable in the basics of manufacturing processes.

Because no women were employed in the Rouge factory before World War II, we teenage students were not distracted from the process of learning. Working at a young age in a smoky and dirty foundry with temperatures of 120°F and visibility of 100 feet, I was inspired to believe there must be something better in life through additional education and training. It was so hot and dusty in the factory that my foreman taught me how to chew tobacco and then to spit to clear out the foundry dust as a means of survival. When I came home at night, I no longer resembled a pale young high-school student who was easily bored with inactivity.

4

The Ford Rouge factory, named for its location along the Rouge River, was the world's largest industrial complex in the early 1900s. (From the Collection of Henry Ford Museum and Greenfield Village)

I always thought I was assigned to the hot and dirty foundry because I had called my previous foreman of the pattern shop "an old S.O.B." In my opinion at the time, my comment was justified. I worked for several weeks in the pattern shop, doing menial work such as painting core boxes. I complained to Mr. Reinholz, the tough German foreman, that I should be permitted to make a pattern. He agreed with some reluctance and handed me a blueprint. With much diligence and care, I completed what I thought was a masterpiece and, with great personal pride of accomplishment, presented my pattern to him. Mr. Reinholz must have thought I should be taught humility because he proceeded to take my beautifully polished mahogany pattern and saw it in half, with no explanation! At this point, I spoke my mind. However, in later years when I became an executive of the Ford Motor Company, I had the personal satisfaction of reminding Mr. Reinholz that when I was a teenager, I thought he was "an old S.O.B." With a smile, I told him that I still thought the same of him, but I expressed my appreciation for his patience in training me. I suppose if he had treated me differently, I might have made pattern making my career. The Lord works in mysterious ways.

After completing the high-school formal program and having been exposed to all manufacturing processes, each student was asked to pick a vocation for additional apprentice study. Then the student was assigned to his chosen field of endeavor. By working eight hours daily at his chosen discipline, the student continued his education within the factory school after work hours. Many graduate apprentices continued formal education in the Detroit night colleges to enhance their education or to earn a degree in a different discipline.

In 36 years of activity, the Ford schools graduated approximately 8,000 students. When factories were unionized in the 1940s, the students no longer could work in the factory or perform union production work. Simulated areas of manufacturing were established; unfortunately, these did not permit the important interactions between skilled workers and students. Upon the death of Henry Ford and through the reorganization of Ford Motor Company by Henry Ford II, greater interest was placed on short-term profitability and resulting cost controls. The financial executives of Ford Motor Company prevailed in the decision to close the school. The executives also recognized that General Motors and Chrysler had developed post-high-school institutes to train future technicians and engineers. The consensus of the prevailing management group was that such training programs should apply to post-high-school students. In today's environment, great evidence remains that hands-on training should be available as part of the high-school curriculum for those students who become restless with an overabundance of formal schooling.

Henry Ford should be given great credit for his concern for educating young people to better prepare them for the real world of work. He was uninhibited by financial and legal interests, and his mission seemed to be one of providing opportunity to those who needed help in bettering their lifestyles. This vision, plus that of making automobiles available to the working man, was responsible for creating a new lifestyle for the multitudes.

Henry Ford's educational program also was unique because it cost taxpayers nothing. It was unlike many of the current enormous federal welfare programs that have proven costly and unsuccessful. Fortunately, the practical value of early vocation selection and the social concern and commitment of industry are receiving great interest. The dire needs of industry for employees who have improved vocational-technical and communication skills are challenging our educators and governmental leaders to place more emphasis on funding new approaches to educating our young people. Increasing importance is being placed on business and industry to partner with community colleges in an effort to support the necessary costly teaching aids to train their future work force. With the rapid increases in technology, special certificates are being issued to recognize the training prescribed by industry and business.

Henry Ford was convinced that young people, similar to adults, would delight in feeling useful and productive. He believed young people would learn faster and develop more self-confidence if their schooling encompassed real problems, instead of locking them in a fantasy world of the classroom for 15 or more years. Henry Ford also believed that "true education consists of learning by doing." He established a school for poor or orphaned boys inside his factories to prove his philosophy. More importantly, Henry Ford took a personal interest in the school and visited it frequently.

Mr. Ford was a visionary in recognizing the importance of a teaching–learning paradigm that also must be addressed in today's educational process. His learning-centered approach established the teacher as the content source, but not the only source of knowledge in the classroom. Interaction of students in classroom and work environments provided an important understanding of how their studies applied to the real world of work.

Chapter 2

Meeting My Mentor

Through my Ford Trade and Apprentice School experience and my interest in engineering, I was assigned to the Ford Engineering Laboratory at Dearborn, where Henry Ford prevailed. I had great anticipation of meeting Mr. Ford. Fortunately, my boss, Larry Sheldrick, recognized I could print very well, and thus I was asked to help Mr. Ford's librarian, a lovely lady named Rachael McDonald, in cataloguing the many books donated to Greenfield Village.

Thousands of Early American books and manuals had been contributed to the Greenfield Village library, and Miss McDonald was overwhelmed in sorting and cataloguing the items. She counseled me to be polite to Mr. Ford when he appeared and to never refer to him as Henry because he was not on a first-name basis with any top management or employees.

During one of Mr. Ford's many visits to the library, during the construction of the Henry Ford Museum and Greenfield Village, Mr. Ford recognized that I was a Trade School student because of the little beanie I wore as a headpiece. Trade School students were required to have short hair and to wear a beanie to prevent their hair from becoming caught in machinery. At that time, it was interesting to me to observe that Francis Jehl, Thomas Edison's superintendent, also wore the little covering. This was a carry-over of early practice to ensure safety from belt-driven machinery. Mr. Ford watched as I took a camel-hair brush and white enamel and carefully numbered the many antique books according to the Dewey decimal system. Of the thousands of books donated to the museum, Mr. Ford's favorite seemed to be the *McGuffey Readers*, which he felt were so important to his early training. He seemed to prefer a book of a size that he could carry in his pocket. The readers were in great supply, and many were used later for the primary grades after Mr. Ford established the Greenfield Village school system. As Mr. Ford leafed through a well-worn reader, he reflected on how the stories always taught principles of right and wrong, both ethical and moral. In particular, one manual taught the importance of taking care of animals and wildlife. As he left, Mr. Ford handed me McGuffey's third eclectic reader and opened it to lesson XXIV. He suggested I read this as being typical of these books. The story is titled "Beautiful Hands." Permit me to share this story with you now:

> "O Miss Roberts! What coarse-looking hands Mary has!" said Daisy Marvin, as she walked home from school with her teacher.
>
> "In my opinion, Daisy, Mary's hands are the prettiest in the class."
>
> "Why Miss Roberts, they are as red and hard as they can be. How they would look if she were to try to play on a piano!" exclaimed Daisy.
>
> Miss Roberts took Daisy's hands in hers and said, "Your hands are very soft and white, Daisy—just the hands to look beautiful on a piano; yet they lack one beauty that Mary's hands have. Shall I tell you what the difference is?"
>
> "Yes, please, Miss Roberts."
>
> "Well, Daisy, Mary's hands are always busy. They wash dishes, they make fires, they hang out clothes, and help to wash them, too; they sweep, and dust, and sew; they are always trying to help her poor, hard-working mother. Besides, they wash and dress the children; they mend their toys and dress their dolls; yet, they find time to bathe the head of the little girl who is so sick in the next house to theirs. They are full of good deeds to every living thing. I have seen them patting the tired horse and the lame dog in the street. They are always ready to help those who need help."
>
> "I shall never think Mary's hands are ugly any more, Miss Roberts."

"I am glad to hear you say that they are beautiful because
they do their work gladly and cheerfully."

"O Miss Roberts! I feel so ashamed of myself, and so sorry,"
said Daisy, looking into her teacher's face with tearful eyes.

"Then my dear, show your sorrow by deeds of kindness.
The good alone are really beautiful."

I was so impressed that, when Mr. Ford left, I continued to read the book until Miss McDonald told me to continue my work. After all, they were paying me 13 cents an hour. I probably was overpaid because I could scan through books of interest when Miss McDonald was not present.

In visiting the Greenfield Village library recently, I was astounded to find the printing on the books has weathered well after approximately 68 years. The current librarian indicated that the Dewey decimal system for cataloguing is still being used; however, a computer paste-on has replaced the camel-hair brush and white ink. Just think—a skill replaced by a computer!

Mr. Ford's great personal interest in 1929 was the development of the Henry Ford Museum and Greenfield Village, whereby he could teach history by observation. He had been quoted as saying, "History is bunk," which really reflected his observation of the written word and its many interruptions by historians. Mr. Ford believed that much of history that was recorded from archival material or word of mouth reflected the writer's interpretation. He believed that a better way of educating the public about important historical events was to create and present the situations or materials in a physical modem that would be preserved. This would permit the viewer to better understand the nuances of the period of history.

At tremendous personal effort and expense by Mr. Ford, Henry Ford Museum and Greenfield Village in Dearborn, Michigan, now stands in all its nostalgic glory for the delight of those interested in Early Americana. During its construction, it was a great delight for me to look out the library window and observe the many artisans reconstructing the historical buildings that had been acquired by Mr. Ford. The village covers approximately 200 acres, with a focal point being the museum.

11

This building is an exact reproduction of the Independence Hall of Philadelphia. Visitors are astounded at the size of the building (440 by 800 feet).

Mr. Ford spared no expense in the building construction. I watched as the museum flooring of teakwood from Burma was laid by experts. This material is resistant to water and rust, and its surface takes a high polish similar to a dance floor. After 70 years of use, the flooring shows little distress from the multitudes that have traveled over it. Upon this beautiful flooring is displayed an unlimited variety of antiques that were donated or acquired. Mr. Ford directed that all articles should be restored to as close as original condition as possible. Artisans from all over the world were brought in to work on restoring these items. As would be obvious, wood-workers, cabinet makers, machinists, tinsmiths, gunsmiths, and all the skilled trades and artisans of the early years were required to return the articles to original working condition. Mr. Ford also wanted to be able to operate the displays. Even the large locomotive mounted on rails and surrounded by the teakwood flooring was driven into the museum. The displays cover a labyrinth of Early Americana items—from a large steam-generating plant to small household items. Every visitor will find his or her area of interest covered in great detail and interestingly displayed.

The exhibits depict advances in science and handicraft, and they cover the various phases of development of engineering, mechanical devices, and useful arts of the earlier periods of history. Adjoining the Philadelphia Independence Hall, the village is another museum of Early Americana historic buildings in a setting typical of that period.

The original red schoolhouse that Mr. Ford attended stands near the court-house where Abraham Lincoln practiced law. A fire lit by Herbert Hoover in 1929 burns perpetually in the same courthouse fireplace where Lincoln warmed himself. As is typical of most Early American settlements, there is a Town Hall facing a Commons. Across the way is the Martha-Mary Chapel, used at the time by Dearborn school children for early morning services. Mr. Ford frequently visited the school and participated in the chapel services.

The many buildings of Greenfield Village, such as Stephen Foster's home, Abraham Lincoln's Courthouse, and the Cotswold Cottage (where Mary of the "Mary Had a Little Lamb" nursery rhyme might have resided), were of

*The Martha-Mary Chapel at Greenfield Village: Exterior view (top)
and interior view (bottom).*

Cotswold cottage in Greenfield Village, where Mary of the nursery rhyme "Mary Had a Little Lamb" might have resided.

keen interest to me as they were being reassembled. At tremendous cost, these buildings had been disassembled piece by piece and then were reconstructed in the Village.

My favorite building has always been Thomas Edison's Menlo Park Laboratory that houses his many experiments in development of the light bulb. Through Mr. Ford's close relationship with Thomas Edison, Mr. Ford had convinced Edison to transfer his Menlo Park Laboratory to Greenfield Village. During my lunch breaks, I had the opportunity to visit both Mr. Edison and his superintendent, Francis Jehl, in the final stages of reestablishing his laboratory at Greenfield Village. Upon completion, Mr. Ford asked Edison what he thought about the appearance compared to his recollection. Edison indicated it was an excellent restoration—except it was more tidy than when he worked in it.

(Left to right) Thomas Edison, Henry Ford, and Francis Jehl in Edison's Menlo Park Laboratory at the dedication of Greenfield Village in 1929. (From the Collection of Henry Ford Museum and Greenfield Village)

As a curious teenager, I was interested in the activities of the two elder statesmen, and they seemed delighted to share stories of their early trials and tribulations. Although Mr. Edison was almost 80 years old, he was enthused and mentally active with his ongoing experiments. He slumped in his chair and seemed to nap quite a bit, and his rather rumpled appearance camouflaged the genius within him. Mr. Jehl indicated that his boss seldom went to bed because he wanted to continue his work at all hours of the day and night when he got a new idea. Even at this point in his life, Mr. Edison was still working on several projects.

After the reconstruction of the Edison laboratory was completed, Francis Jehl continued to entertain visitors there and delighted in telling of his earlier experiences with Edison. He seemed to be recapturing his early life and sensing that his former boss remained by his side.

One of the last major projects on which Edison worked was an attempt to develop artificial rubber from plant life. This project resulted from the association of Mr. Ford and his camping buddies, Thomas Edison and Harvey Firestone. At one of their camping sojourns into the Appalachian Mountains, they discussed their concern about a projected shortage of natural rubber from Malaysia.

During World War I, natural rubber was a critical material for defense. Mr. Ford had been experimenting with development of fibers from plant life, and he and Firestone suggested Edison might find a plant that would produce resin for production of artificial rubber. Edison established a laboratory at Fort Myers, Florida, and started a concentrated search for the best plant that would produce the greatest amount of resin. Mr. Ford built a home next to Edison's home in Fort Myers to keep in touch with him and to watch his progress. Edison had the railroad workers collect plant-life samples from all over the eastern part of the United States for his experiment. He collected 3,227 wild plants and shrubs from the whole East Coast. He continued the search until more than 14,000 plants were analyzed for potential rubber resin. Edison finally fixed on goldenrod, which yielded approximately five percent resin. Through plant selection and crossbreeding, a giant goldenrod was developed to produce twelve percent resin. Before the project could become commercial, the European chemists discovered they could make artificial rubber from petroleum products at much less cost. With Edison's death, Mr. Ford never again visited his Fort Myers home. He missed his mentor, whose major concern was inventing things the world needed.

The Henry Ford Museum and Greenfield Village is located next to the Product Engineering Building of Ford Motor Company (now called the EEE building), where Mr. Ford had his office and where I finally was assigned. Much to my delight, this permitted me to continue my visits to Greenfield Village during lunch periods and to observe the unfolding of this panorama of Early American history.

Aerial view of the Henry Ford Museum, showing the EEE Engineering Laboratory in the upper left corner. (From the Collection of Henry Ford Museum and Greenfield Village)

As already mentioned, every effort was made to assure that traditions of the display were as exact as possible. For instance, Mr. Ford wanted lambs grazing within Greenfield Village, in the same way that Mary of "Mary Had a Little Lamb" would have enjoyed. A beautiful green lawn surrounding the museum was provided for the enjoyment of the lambs. This created quite a pastoral scene as the lambs grazed peacefully.

One day as I walked toward Greenfield Village, I noticed to my great dismay that, for some reason, the lambs had been shorn of their tails and no longer could wag them. When I pointed this out to Mr. Ford, he was furious and quickly instructed the farm manager to put the tails back on the lambs! The next day, new lambs with tails were grazing peacefully on the lawn. During a recent visit to Greenfield Village, I observed with some regret that concrete parking lots have replaced the lambs' pasture area.

With the completion of Greenfield Village, a public education system was made available for a select number of primary grade students of the area. Mr. Ford delighted in visiting with the young students and teachers, and he spent many hours joining in the chapel services and classrooms, thus assuring that the education process duplicated his early childhood experiences.

Mr. Ford particularly enjoyed the students' musical programs. Having acquired several expensive Stradivarius and Cremona violins, he had a habit of loaning them to certain students. Mr. Ford indicated the violins needed use to preserve them. This was accepted; however, the custodian of the violins had great difficulty in keeping track of which students were using the violins because Mr. Ford would forget to notify the caretaker.

Mr. Ford seemed to love association with young people because they were not threatening or demanding. He indicated to me that the excitement and energy of young people could be contagious and rehabilitating, compared to the mundane problems of adults. I have found this truism and early lesson to have influenced my lifestyle. Helping to offer educational opportunities to young people has taken most of my spare time, and the rewards continue to keep me young at heart.

Chapter 3

First Impressions

The Product Engineering Laboratory (now called the EEE building) and Henry Ford's executive office were but a stone's throw from the Henry Ford Museum and Greenfield Village. This was the hub of Mr. Ford's daily activities during his reign in the 1920s until his death in 1947. The facility was within walking distance of Mr. Ford's Fair Lane residence. His home and his office at the Engineering Laboratory reflected his desire for simple accommodations rather than the typical grandeur of his wealthy peers. The laboratory and offices compose a formidable building that originally was designed as a typical saw-tooth-roof-type factory with railroad tracks down the middle.

In 1924, Mr. Ford added an office complex to the front of the EEE Product Engineering building. The structure is the typical gray limestone facade found in governmental buildings. After approximately seven decades, the building remains impressive and offers a feeling of perpetuity. Henry Ford and his limited staff conducted daily activities from these offices. At the time, if you gazed out the window, you could enjoy the beautiful scene of a placid lake surrounded by many trees, shrubs, and an abundance of waterfowl, birds, and small wildlife. Mr. Ford had a telescope in his office and another in his home to enable him to do bird-watching. He loved birds and had 400 birdbaths throughout his Fair Lane property.

The factory's original purpose was changed by removing the railroad tracks that ran through the middle of the building. The long expansive area was finished with beautiful highly polished hard oak flooring. The only obstructions to the expansive open area were large roof-supporting columns that had been plastered to a round form to eliminate the harshness of typical steel beams. Two of these pillars are most notable to me because they identify events of historical importance that will be mentioned later.

The EEE Engineering Laboratory and Henry Ford's office.

When I joined Ford Motor Company at the end of the 1920s, the Product Engineering activities were performed by approximately 250 individuals. This included designers, development staff, and the necessary skilled trades to produce experimental parts and to test vehicles and components. This filled only a small portion of the expansive building. A large open area existed between Mr. Ford's front office and the engineers' area. This buffer zone enabled us to watch for Mr. Ford's arrival each morning and be certain everyone was busy.

The classic Model A was in production at the time, and work was commencing on the new Model B and the first V8 engine. This period of automotive history was unusual because it reflects the stock market crash of October 1929 and the bank holidays of the early 1930s. With banks closed, downsizing was occurring in great proportions in the industry. When this occurred, the Product Engineering Department was reduced to five employees. Being an apprentice, I did not add much to the overhead and thus was permitted to retain my job. Although Edsel Ford was a director of the bank where Ford had its funds, the only money available for payroll was a special safe at the Ford administration building adjoining the Rouge factory. Therefore, payroll was limited.

The top management was led by Henry Ford, who was absolute boss but had no official title. His son Edsel was considered president but had little decision-making authority. Charles Sorensen was in charge of worldwide manufacturing and had no title; however, Sorensen took his orders directly from Henry Ford and was responsible for implementing them, although Mr. Ford often gave directives to other managers or lesser employees as well. Lawrence Sheldrick had no title but was in charge of product engineering, and Harry Bennett likewise had no title but was in charge of personnel functions, including factory security. Bennett had a large work force throughout the organization to spy on individuals and to report to Mr. Ford. This espionage system will be discussed in more detail in a later chapter.

It may be difficult for young readers to grasp how a large corporation such as Ford Motor Company could operate with only a few nonproduction employees and only a handful of management. Some of these early experiences may help readers understand how large corporations operated with so few employees, before the advent of today's complex and large corporate structures.

My first assignment in Product Engineering was that of operating a wet grinder to finish an experimental part. The small machine shop was not far from Henry Ford's front office. Mr. Ford had visited with me previously at Greenfield Village and had spotted me on his daily visit to the experimental shop. Unfortunately for me, I thought it rather macho to chew tobacco as the tough foundry workers had taught me to do. Because the machine I was operating had a liquid-cooling solution to cool the metal while grinding, I thought it convenient to spit into the solution because no one would notice the difference.

I had forgotten that Henry Ford's mentor, Thomas Edison, had convinced Mr. Ford that the use of tobacco, particularly smoking, degenerated the mind, and thus its use by Ford employees was not permitted. As Mr. Ford approached me that day, I knew I was in big trouble. The chaw was going to become bigger with time, and I had no way to relieve myself until Mr. Ford left. It must have been obvious to Mr. Ford that I was chewing tobacco, so he waited until I finally had to swallow. This cured me of the habit of chewing tobacco, and it was a lesson well learned.

I have always thought that Thomas Edison had an extraordinary sense of observation and many firm beliefs without scientific proof. It is remarkable that with today's science, many of Edison's theories now can be proven. Edison thought the practice of rolling a cigarette in paper tissue and inhaling the smoke had serious effects on the brain. Note that Edison's observation about the harmful effects of tobacco was the reason the early Ford cars did not have ashtrays. Henry Ford felt he should not encourage his customers to use tobacco. Sixty-five years later, the tobacco industry and the automotive industry now have sufficient scientific proof that Edison and Ford were true visionaries.

Although Henry Ford did not permit the use of tobacco on the premises when I began working at Ford Motor Company, in earlier years he permitted a character named Spider Huff to use snuff. Henry Ford had hired Huff because he was knowledgeable about magnetos and Mr. Ford needed this skill for the Model T development. I was told that Spider Huff came from the hills of Tennessee, wearing a typical dress of bib overalls and tennis shoes. With Huff also came his favorite rocking chair and his spittoon. Often, Huff would be rocking in his chair while visiting with Henry Ford, and he would project a spray toward the vessel and at times would miss his target, much to Henry Ford's dismay. Huff also irritated the development engineers because he would be testing a car and forget to roll down the window when he wanted to relieve himself. The resulting mess was similar to spraying a liquid window cleaner on the car windows, except not as tidy. Finally, the testing staff put a funnel outlet through the floor boards of Huff's car, thus saving window-cleaning effort.

As I became better acquainted with Henry Ford, I soon recognized that his lifestyle was simple and uncomplicated. He seemed to have an insatiable curiosity about nature and mechanical things. This drove him and his associates to unlimited lengths to delve into the mysteries of such things. It seemed as if nothing had happened before Henry Ford's arrival that challenged him to explore these things to his own satisfaction. He would not accept the judgment of the so-called "more learned" people that something would not work. He had to prove it to himself. For instance, Henry Ford would get the idea that farm roads could be improved by making a machine that would pick up the gravel, mix it with concrete and water, and relay it. None of his engineers was brave enough to say this would not work. A machine was made, and the experiment was tried. Obviously, it failed because the aggregate was unpredictable. Fortunately, Henry Ford was never discouraged by such failures.

Henry Ford and his friend and mentor, Thomas Edison, took no stock in printed knowledge of that era. They had to convince themselves that what seemed impossible, to the learned world, might be accomplished. Neither man would have accepted the theory that "the cow could not jump over the moon," as the riddle declared it could. They would have said we are not sure unless we explore it ourselves. As we know today, their logic was correct. We now have proven that a man can be placed on the moon. Their early observations of printed knowledge and its rate of obsolescence were perceptive. With today's rapid advances in technology, many textbooks are obsolete before they hit the marketplace.

Both Henry Ford and Thomas Edison believed that too much formal education would inhibit the technician or engineer from original thinking. This attitude induced those with formal degrees to never discuss their wisdom obtained from books or to indicate that a project was not feasible because of theories derived from book learning.

The typical experiment of Edison—trying 10,000 different experiments to determine the best material for his light-bulb filament—exemplifies the thinking of these two pioneers. As you may recall, Edison never became depressed with his failures because he indicated that he learned something from all 9,999 failures.

Henry Ford was a great visionary with a childlike enthusiasm to explore new ideas to his own satisfaction. He was not oriented only toward profit, nor was he inhibited by pressures from stockholders, as is typical of chief operating officers today. Likewise, Henry Ford was not inhibited by lawyers and financiers who readily point out the challenges of free thinking. He also was not influenced by a great circle of close friends or those in whom he might confide. His circle of friends was limited, and socializing was secondary to his interest in new developments.

Henry Ford seemed uncomfortable in large group activities and preferred association with a small group of product development and manufacturing staff. Because he had a rather complex personality, at that time we had great difficulty in anticipating his next move or his reaction to our suggestions. Mr. Ford seemed to delight in keeping others guessing about what his next move might be. As a teenager, I thought Mr. Ford was a bit mischievous. He certainly was not inhibited by anyone, and I don't think he understood himself. It was as if he were caught in a lifestyle that forced him to be something he was not. It impressed me that Mr. Ford wanted a simple lifestyle and less pressure to place him into a public mold that did not fit him. He recognized that he must appear as a tough decision maker; however, his temperament never equipped him for such a position.

As a young person, I suppose I found Henry Ford to be the antithesis of the mean-spirited things with which he was charged. To appear tough, others such as Harry Bennett and Charles Sorensen (who spent considerable time with Henry Ford) took advantage of this timidity and convinced him of the need to be tough with others. Although Henry Ford was not a saint, he certainly was not the blackguard that many have portrayed him to be. Most of Henry Ford's close working associates, including top managers, had great difficulty in second-guessing him. Because of Mr. Ford's unpredictable behavior, none of those working with him could claim close or friendly relationships with him. His social life was limited and of his own choosing, and he seldom met with his few top managers on a social basis.

In his latter years, Henry Ford seemed to distrust adults, as if he suspected they had ulterior motives; however, he seemed comfortable with young people, as I discovered in my teenage years. Although my older associates were somewhat afraid of Mr. Ford, I delighted in how he operated and felt rather secure as a trainee.

Henry Ford could appear harsh, but he would relax at times and ask Sorensen to pull out his harmonic and play a tune for us. Mr. Ford also carried a jew's-harp in his pocket and would join in the music. We enjoyed this moment of frivolity, but when I later tried playing the jew's-harp, I found it almost knocked out my teeth. This little instrument was placed in the mouth and stroked to make it vibrate similar to a tuning fork.

Mr. Ford always carried in his pockets the typical things of a young person—a handkerchief, a jew's-harp, a knife, a comb, some twine, and no money. He never felt money was important in his life. He never was burdened with paper and abhorred those who found it necessary. He did carry a little notebook and pencil for jogging his memory, and he told me that a pocket file was all that one should maintain for daily activities.

Henry Ford's personal lifestyle and habits were of great interest to me as a teenager. He was a billionaire with utter disregard for personal desires. He would spend millions on projects of interest and the best production machinery, but he was reluctant to spend money on his personal needs. However, Mr. Ford was always neat, and his clothing was well pressed. Although he appeared prosperous, he never seemed to have any money with him and would borrow a nickel for a candy bar. This was particularly interesting to me because I was told that when the United States Post Office developed a stamp recognizing the fiftieth anniversary of Thomas Edison's invention of the light bulb, Henry Ford accompanied Edison to the ceremony. A few commemorative stamps were made available to those present, and Henry Ford had to borrow two cents from Edison to purchase his stamp.

Although Henry Ford was frugal in spending money on personal pleasures, he always dressed tastefully, and his shoes always shined. One day as he was chatting with Larry Sheldrick, I noticed Mr. Ford had a hole in his shoe sole. I pointed this out to Mr. Ford, and he indicated that the shoes were broken in and very comfortable. He said he was reluctant to replace them but would have them resoled.

On another occasion, during one of my field trips to the Fair Lane estate farm (which today is the site of a large shopping center), Mr. Ford and I were walking in a field of harvested corn. It was a wintry day in late November, and the stalks were cut just above the surface and frozen. (This was before the day of combines.) As we sauntered across the field, I caught my nice teenager argyle sock on a sharp stalk and got a run in it. I showed the run to Mr. Ford, and he said to me, "Young man, you should wear black socks like mine, and you would be able to match them up without throwing away the pair." I complimented him on this advice, whereupon he continued by stating, "Mrs. Ford darns my socks when they get a hole in them." Furthermore, he confided that Mrs. Ford was a lumpy darner and that the socks were not too comfortable. In his considerate and sensitive way, he admitted that he never mentioned this inadequacy to Mrs. Ford because she had the best of intentions as a dutiful wife. However, it was amusing to me that when Mr. Ford's housemaid, Rosa Buhler, passed away several years after Henry Ford, many new pairs of men's socks were found in his room, which had been hidden by Mr. Ford without his wife's knowledge. Apparently, Rosa Buhler knew about Mr. Ford's desire for undarned socks.

As a teenager making 13 cents per hour during the Great Depression, I suggested to Mr. Ford how difficult it was for me to meet my obligations to the family and still have enough money to take my girlfriend to a movie and have a snack. Mr. Ford asked if I liked my work, whereupon I replied, "Yes, it is enjoyable, and I am learning a great deal." His counsel was that money was not important, as long as you liked your work. He prophesied that if I worked hard and applied myself, money would always be available to take care of my needs. Furthermore, Mr. Ford said that if you liked your work, that work would be pleasant and you would be successful. His prediction came true for me, and I never forgot his advice. In 1940 when Henry Ford II became a trainee in Product Engineering, I had the opportunity to offer him the same advice as his grandfather had given me. I suggested that if he worked hard and applied himself, he would succeed. Of course, we all knew Henry Ford II would advance beyond his beginning salary.

Although Mr. Ford was rather frugal on personal matters, I found that Mrs. Ford did appreciate spending more freely on one occasion. The Fords usually went south during the late winter months to the Richmond Hill Plantation near Savannah, Georgia, and they remained there until spring. One winter, I was fortunate to accompany the drivers transporting the Fords' luggage, and I enjoyed the experience. The drivers said that the usual plan was to go by way of Cleveland, Tennessee, because they could obtain a hotel room for the Fords for three dollars per night.

In the early 1930s, highways across the mountains seemed to have been laid out from previous cow paths and Indian trails. They were not graded or maintained well. Unfortunately, the timing of our trip was such that the mountains were covered with snowed and were impassable. We decided to travel around the mountains by way of Cincinnati, Ohio; thus, no reservations had been made for night accommodations. Therefore, we arrived at the most prestigious hotel of the day, the Netherland Plaza. Upon inquiring about a room for the Fords, we learned that the hotel was completely booked except for the bridal suite. We had no other options and thus decided to rent the $30-per-night suite for the Fords and to "take our lumps" when Mr. Ford asked us about the price. The drivers and I spent the night in a low-cost boarding house down the street.

We arose early the next morning, planning how we would approach the Fords about their expensive accommodations. We agreed that the best approach was to ask Mrs. Ford how she liked the room. Her response was, "It was one of the finest hotel rooms I have experienced." This was followed by Mr. Ford asking what we had to pay for the room. When we told him it was $30 for the night, he replied that this sum represented the value of almost 100 bushels of corn. He seemed peeved at us for the remainder of the journey. This taught me to relate hotel bills to the price of a bushel of corn. With current prices, the relationship remains valid today.

The Cleveland, Tennessee, route to Georgia also was of enthusiastic interest to Henry Ford because the route snaked in and out of many areas that had antiques for sale. The winding roads did not permit fast travel, which was appealing to Mr. Ford because the drivers could stop along the way whenever a likely collection for the Greenfield Village might be obtained. At times, Mr. Ford would make an offer for the entire collection, much to the astonishment of the owner.

Because Henry Ford was not much for socializing and his lifestyle was simple and uncomplicated, he was a homebody who seldom attended formal gatherings. In the 1930s, when Henry Ford was becoming nostalgic about the fun-filled days of his youth, he suggested to his wife, Clara Ford, that they try to recapture some of the fun of their early years. The couple had enjoyed early ballroom dancing with their young friends. Thus, in his usual thorough way, Mr. Ford searched and found the most outstanding master of music and dance that was typical of the era of his younger life. Benjamin Lovett from the eastern United States was convinced to come to Dearborn with his musicians, and they first were housed in one end of the EEE Engineering Laboratory. Much to the consternation of the workers, the musicians practiced during the day. We probably were the first engineering activity to have direct rather than piped-in background music.

Henry Ford was convinced that his managers and employees at the Engineering Laboratory should learn the graceful and courteous gestures of ballroom dancing. He believed this would remove some of the rough edges from our daily lifestyle. Most of us were as graceful as pigs on ice. Furthermore, with our work schedule, we had little appreciation of the need for ballroom courtesies. Nonetheless, we were asked to join the dance lessons after work on a weekly basis.

Henry and Clara Ford danced to the music of Benjamin Lovett.
(From the Collection of Henry Ford Museum and Greenfield Village)

I vividly remember I was instructed during the lessons to hold my girlfriend at arm's length and to bow with graceful movements. This did not impress me because it seemed more natural to hold my girlfiend very close as she was a better dancer and it was the practice of the young set of the day. Clara and Henry Ford were fine dancers and thoroughly enjoyed dancing to the music of their youth. Both were unusually nimble and graceful for their age, and the experience permitted the small engineering staff to enjoy Mr. Ford's company. It also convinced me that I needed a bit of polishing of the rough spots of behavior that I had acquired from working with the tough factory supervisors.

As a teenager, these early impressions had a lasting effect on me and convinced me that I had much to learn from Mr. Ford and the senior staff. Little did I realize that a major corporation could be operated by so few decision makers. I soon knew that I was fortunate to be a part of a small group of the most capable engineers and a strong leader. Their counseling and role modeling helped me develop. Although I considered myself a streetwise teenager, I now realize that my immediate supervisor, Larry Sheldrick (in charge of Product Engineering), was a great tutor. He kept advising me to "Keep your mouth shut and listen. You can't learn while you are talking."

Chapter 4

Early Organizational Structure

As previously mentioned, Ford Motor Company had no organizational chart in the 1930s. Henry Ford did consider his son Edsel as president, and all other key executives were considered in charge of some activity but had no title. Assignments could change rather rapidly, depending on the whim of the boss. Henry Ford believed that an organizational chart inhibited flexibility of assignment of the work force. He also indicated that his greatest competitor, General Motors, had many vice presidents and titles, similar to other major corporations. Henry Ford observed that with such an organizational structure, you could not comfortably reduce the number of staff without firing your golfing or fishing buddies. Furthermore, without bureaucratic organizational charts, Ford Motor Company operations would require one-on-one direct supervision by all concerned, thereby minimizing paperwork. Henry Ford believed that one could manage a business, but people had to be led by direct contact. He always impressed upon us that cars were built by people, not paper; therefore, the process did not justify extensive paperwork and legal talent. Henry Ford kept close tabs on the number of nonproduction workers (i.e., those who were not producing a part of the car) and nonproduction salary employees. Relatively speaking, his staff was always small. After the bank holiday in 1933, Mr. Ford's personal staff consisted of a secretary, a legal counselor, one patent lawyer, a librarian, and a few clerical staff. His son Edsel presided in a multi-story office building adjoining the Rouge factory. Marketing, purchasing, transportation, personnel, and other clerical activities also were housed at this location.

Henry Ford kept a wary eye on limiting the number of financial staff. Edsel Ford recognized the dire need to maintain better financial records and tried desperately to establish a group to bring improved controls at Ford Motor Company. In this effort, Edsel hired several staff while his father was overseas. Unfortunately, Henry Ford's spy, Harry Bennett, reported the hirings to Henry Ford. This resulted in Edsel having to cover his tracks by transferring the new staff to other activities.

Henry Ford believed that legal and finance staff served no purpose except to add cost and to prevent forward movement on projects. His theory was that legal and finance people always left a doubt about the wisdom of moving ahead with a project because of legal implications or cost effectiveness. Henry Ford believed that with his style of management, projects could be completed, accepted, or rejected before the naysayers could express their opinions. This style of management was most effective in its time and permitted a flexibility of assignments to various development people, without outside influence. Henry Ford often would assign two groups from different areas of the company to work independently on the same project to ensure that he had alternate solutions to the problem.

Henry Ford probably was the first industry leader to recognize that workers' and management's wages should not vary substantially. He often indicated that workers had the same basic needs as management, and thus the incomes of the two groups should be approximately the same. An interesting observation results if you compare a typical organizational chart of today, which has many levels of supervision, with Henry Ford's lack of an organizational chart and only a handful of executives in his company. Ford's early executives' salaries were approximately double the workers' wages. In today's typical large industry, salary levels increase geometrically with each step upward in an organizational chart. Thus, if the lowest paid worker earns $40,000 per year, each step up the organizational chart increases, until the top chief operating executive may reach $4,000,000. This depends on how many supervisors, managers, vice presidents, group vice presidents, executive vice presidents, and other management staff have been determined to be necessary. Too often, it is based on having similar structures for like corporations. After many years as part of the system, I believe that the same organizational and salary consultants used by the industry have provided a basis for having the blind lead the blind. This seems to be an accepted practice; however, I believe it is somewhat self-serving for those who hire the consultants.

Although Henry Ford kept a tight reign on nonproduction employees (i.e., those not producing a car part), he employed more help than seemed necessary to ensure that the Engineering Laboratory and factories were spotless. The large expanse of hard oak flooring at the laboratory was polished daily, and the machine tools were kept carefully in perfect order. Henry Ford was meticulous in his personal habits and believed that an environment of orderliness would encourage quality output. The Ford factories were always clean and free of clutter. Henry Ford once told my boss, Lawrence Sheldrick, that he felt it a better investment to hire extra help for maintaining the cleanliness of the factory facilities than to send profits to the government to be wasted on nonproductive activities.

As I mentioned previously, Lawrence Sheldrick was my boss and was in charge of Product Engineering. He had no title but obtained his orders from either Henry Ford or Charles Sorensen. Sorensen was in charge of worldwide manufacturing and, in an organizational structure of today, would be considered chief operating officer. Edsel Ford was president of Ford Motor Company, but he made no major decisions without his father's approval. There was no doubt in anyone's mind who was the real boss of the company. The organization of Ford Motor Company in 1938 still is exemplified by one of the historical pillars located in the EEE building.

I was present when Larry Sheldrick, Henry Ford, and other top management visited the large open area of the Engineering Laboratory in the EEE building. Henry Ford wanted to see who was the tallest of the group of management staff. We had them take turns standing against the pillar, and we recorded their heights.

Sixty years later, I returned to my "haunt" of the past to see what had happened to this particular pillar. In approaching this facility, I reflected on how I used to park in front of the building in a reserved parking spot. I still had my key to the front lobby door and for the executive lavatory in the front of the building. I wondered if these would give me access into the building. As would be expected, in the lobby was a pretty young receptionist. I am sure she thought, "Who is this old coot, and what does he want?" She asked with whom I wanted to visit, and I politely told her my friends were long gone but that I knew Louis Ross, a current executive vice president. Ross used to be my newsboy and was a bright and ambitious young man. I believe this impressed her. Therefore,

I continued to plead my case, telling her I had come all the way from Iowa to satisfy my curiosity about what had happened to the building and its historical pillars.

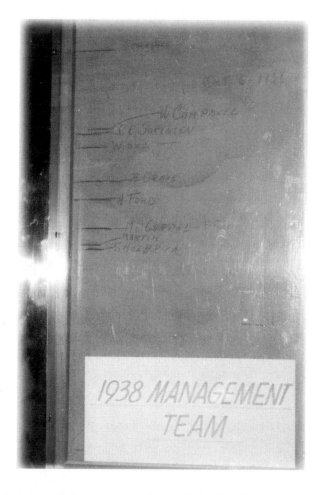

The heights of the nine members of the Ford Motor Company management team in 1938 are marked on a pillar in the EEE Product Engineering building and can still be found there today.

The receptionist had never heard of the history behind the pillars and questioned that they even existed. She was not acquainted with the history of the building. Because I probably appeared somewhat unthreatening and, I suppose to her, similar to Rip Van Winkle returning from a long sleep, the receptionist finally permitted me take a quick look. Lo! And behold! As I entered the main building, the former wide-open space had been transformed into a maze of small offices through which I rather apprehensively threaded my way. It struck me that activities of today require engineers to become isolated from each other. The wide-open area of this building, with the little desk in the middle, was a thing of the past. The maze of small cubicles and corridors did not permit you to spot a person or have a direct route, as was the case with Henry Ford. As I wended my way through the maze and inquired about the pillar, it became obvious to me that history was not a subject of interest to those accomplishing their daily tasks at the facility.

After considerable searching, I finally found the pillar. Some thoughtful person, with a sense of historical concern, had placed a picture frame over the height markings and had listed the display as the "1938 management team." As I reflected on the earlier occasion, a busy young man with blueprints under his arm paused and asked about the display. I explained how the company in 1938 had only nine men listed as management and that my boss, Larry Sheldrick, was shown as the shortest. Furthermore, the building was mostly vacant at that time long ago, and the pillar had stood out then. The young man was not impressed by my story, and he pardoned himself to continue with his work. As I tried to find my way back to the lobby, I reflected on how we used to look across the huge expanse of oak flooring to watch Henry Ford sprightfully bounce across the wide-open space, past the lone desk in the middle of the floor, and continue toward the group to share his thoughts for the day.

The desk in the middle of the floor was a reception point when our few engineers visited with potential suppliers. I well remember the occasion when a young product application engineer from Holley Carburetor visited me. His name was Milt Kittler, and he had a little updraft carburetor (which cost $1.75) that he wanted me to consider for application. Knowing Mr. Ford usually arrived early in the morning and always wanted everyone to be busy, I suggested to Milt that if Mr. Ford should appear, he was to immediately grab a shop towel and to begin polishing one of the experimental cars until Mr. Ford left. Sure enough, Mr. Ford arrived, and Milt jumped up with great energy and started dusting the car. In later years, when Milt Kittler became chairman of the board of Holley Carburetor, he mentioned how he had worked for Ford Motor Company without being on its payroll. I suggested that the lesson of "always being busy" was what made Milt so successful in later years, but it also kept me out of trouble with Henry Ford.

Compared to organizational structures of today, it is amazing how so few could accomplish so much. Having played a part in watching industry geometrically increase the number of nonproduction staff over the years, I now am encouraged to see that industry finally has recognized the urgent need to return to more reasonable levels of paper shufflers. The computer has reduced the need for clerical help and permits instant global communication. Likewise, modern management now recognizes the importance of empowering workers in the decision-making process. This has resulted in continued reduction of staff and a quicker turnaround in the decision-making process.

Although the first pillar in the EEE Ford Engineering Laboratory reflected the organization of Ford Motor Company in 1938, the other pillar of interest to me was one that again reflected the height of Henry Ford and his camping buddies. Although Mr. Ford never had close personal friends, he did consider Thomas Edison as his mentor. Edison was approximately 15 years older than Ford. When Henry Ford began work on his first car, Edison encouraged him to continue and told him he was on the right track toward having a vehicle with its own portable fuel. Edison also told Henry Ford not to let anyone discourage him or sway him from his course. Henry Ford's other camping buddies were Harvey Firestone (of Firestone tires), John Burroughs (the emeritus of natural science), and Luther Burbank (plant scientist and developer of the navel orange). The old Model T with built-in camper served the group for a yearly camping trip in the Smoky Mountains. During the camp-out, Henry Ford would chop the wood for the evening fire, saying he warmed himself twice by cutting the wood. The group were all visionaries, and I am certain the discussions were most interesting. Upon returning to the Ford Engineering Laboratory, someone thought the heights of the camping friends should be recorded on one pillar of the building. During my recent visit to the Ford Engineering Laboratory, I did not have time to find this particular pillar, but I hope it has not been painted over.

Prior to the bank holiday in 1933, Ford Product Engineering was quite small because Mr. Ford was the head project engineer. He took great delight in assigning projects to different individuals. Key Product Engineering supervisors were Lawrence Sheldrick and Joe Galamb. Sheldrick was in charge of the complete vehicle, and Galamb was in charge of the body engineering. In addition to these two key players, Mr. Ford had several old-timers from the Model T era, such as Eugene Farkas, Karl Schultz, Emil Zoerlein, Howard Simpson, and Dale Roeder. He would work with these individuals on advanced ideas. If any of these projects proved feasible, he would have Sheldrick pick up the project and develop it for production. Because Mr. Ford spent considerable time on his special projects, Sheldrick had time to concentrate on getting the production vehicles into production.

The Product Engineering staff at this time was limited. Ford Motor Company expected a large percentage of new ideas to originate from its key suppliers. Briggs and Murray Corporations provided a major portion of the body engineering and had on their staffs a few artisans who had learned their skills from the carriage era. Other major suppliers such as Warner Gear Corporation (supplier of transmissions), Dana (supplier of driveline components), Timken Axle (supplier of axles), Holley Carburetor and Zenith Carburetor (suppliers of carburetors), Gemmer Gear (supplier of steering mechanisms), Bendix and Kelsey Hayes (suppliers of brakes), and others were providing a major part of the research for Ford Motor Company and the industry.

Car body design and engineering as we know it today was in its infancy. Before the 1930s, body building was virtually an art. The knowledge and practices employed resulted from individual skills and experience. Shape and form of sheet metal was simple and kept within the limits of stretching the available material without rupture when using production dies. Designers were limited by production capabilities to form shapes. Difficult shapes still required much hand forming. Typical custom car bodies of the period were mostly hammered by hand over wooden forms. Much soldering and hand filing was required to provide a finished product. During this period, the industry was going from the art of carriage making to an enclosure that would have more aesthetic appeal. Body engineers were somewhat limited because this was a period before plastics and synthetic fibers.

Without an organizational structure, Mr. Ford found it convenient to visit with various areas of operation and to make assignments. This kept his key supervisors hustling to determine how their projects would mesh with his latest thinking. This style of operation provided a bit of competition among individuals having similar assignments. It was obvious to some of us that Mr. Ford was being mischievous and delighted in keeping the group guessing about his next move. For instance, one day Mr. Ford told a young man in Dearborn to go to the head of the purchasing department at the Rouge factory and tell the man he was taking over. Obviously, the head of purchasing was shocked and asked who gave the man his orders. When told it was Mr. Ford, the head of purchasing became more concerned. After many phone calls, Mr. Ford finally admitted he was merely trying to get "a rise" out of the man.

Mr. Ford believed that his mode of operation prevented individuals from building non-invasive bureaucracies within the organization. This also permitted direct one-on-one operation between individuals. Projects could be expedited because all functions could work concurrently on the project. It is interesting to note that today's most alert management groups are finding the benefits of forming project teams to accomplish what Mr. Ford already had in place. These project teams now consist of all disciplines necessary to carry out a project. This method of operation eliminates the great delay in sequentially transferring the project from function to function. More importantly, it builds team spirit and ownership of the project. A much greater reward of this system of operation is the opportunity for the various disciplines to train their peers about their functions. I have always observed that developing the potential of employees is as important as developing a good end project.

Although Mr. Ford's method of operation may seem rather primitive to the modern set, it eliminated paperwork and provided great flexibility of operation.

Chapter 5

Bank Holiday and Downsizing

The bank holiday in 1933 was most memorable because money was not available and thus great downsizing occurred in industry. Henry Ford had encouraged the Trade School students to save money, and he would match it. I had saved $59.73 from my tremendous earnings of 13 cents per hour, and I mentioned to Mr. Ford that my money was locked up by the bank closure. Mr. Ford had a similar problem. Because the company had difficulty meeting the payroll, he had a bank safe at the Dearborn Product Engineering Laboratory for contingency purposes. The unavailability of money resulted in the Product Engineering staff being reduced to five people and me (still a trainee and apparently being paid what I was worth). With so few remaining staff, Larry Sheldrick asked me to help handle the release forms to authorize the product for production in 1933, change the drawings, run the blueprint machine, do the limited filing, and in my spare time help follow-up fabrication of experimental parts. These responsibilities made me feel quite important. Because we had so few staff, Mr. Ford would visit with individuals without the presence of their supervisors. This concerned those in charge because they never knew to what Mr. Ford agreed. My supervisor would always council me about this situation and advise me to be very courteous with Mr. Ford.

One day, Mr. Ford was visiting with me and in a fatherly way suggested that if I needed any answers to problems, I should ask him for help. As a typical streetwise teenager, I thought at the time, "What could he tell me that I don't already know?" I enjoyed these visits and now recognize how fortunate I was in being a part of this small department and having the advice of such a wise man. With the small staff of engineers, you could say it was similar to the days when Mr. Ford had started his company. Mr. Ford's style of one-on-one management continued until his retirement because he felt comfortable working with a small group. However, Product Engineering continued to be understaffed. The size of the group never reached 200 during Henry Ford's regime.

Mr. Ford's typical workday during the early 1930s consisted of coming to the Product Engineering Laboratory office in early morning and telling the group what he had thought we should work on since his last visit. As a typical one-on-one direct supervisor, Mr. Ford would say, "I will be back in the afternoon to see how you are doing." No one dared tell him we were still working on several of his previous suggestions, including some in which we had a personal interest. Mr. Ford's daily attention to Product Engineering kept the small group jumping. When Larry Sheldrick asked for more help, Mr. Ford's reply was that we "didn't need much more than a sketch on an envelope to make a part and test it." With pressure from Charles Sorensen and Edsel Ford, Mr. Ford finally added a few more engineers and technicians to the staff. When the group totaled 25, he found it an advantage because he then could assign the same project to two different individuals in order to have alternate solutions to his suggestions.

After his morning visis to the Product Engineering Laboratory, Mr. Ford would leave with his driver or the farm manager, Ray Dahlinger, to visit his 26,000 acres of farms around Dearborn, or he would go with Charles Sorensen to visit the factory. His trips through the outlying country to inspect the farms often resulted in his interest in purchasing additional farms. Mr. Ford preferred land with a stream running through it, and he envisioned the stream as a potential source of water power for future cottage industries. When Mr. Ford found a likely piece of property of interest, he would ask Dahlinger to check its availability. Frequently, Mr. Ford found that he already owned the farm. Additionally, he spent considerable time watching the development of his pet project, the Henry Ford Museum and Greenfield Village.

During my early training with the staff that had just finished the development of the Model A, I learned a great deal about Mr. Ford's basic design objectives. The old-timers shared many of their experiences regarding their work on the previous Model T and how difficult it was to convince Mr. Ford that he should consider replacing the classic design that had provided low-cost basic transportation for the multitudes. The classic Model T was recognized by competitors as a real challenge because it offered affordable transportation for the average working man.

Mr. Ford resisted changing the classic design that had been so successful. During the rather long life span of the Model T, the competition had learned to develop lower-cost products with added features. With continued pressure from Edsel Ford, Henry Ford finally agreed to provide a more deluxe competitor to the General Motors Chevrolet and the Chrysler Plymouth models. Having finally agreed to Edsel's suggestion, Henry Ford believed he could compete most effectively by adopting the best new materials and features of the competitors' more expensive models and still accomplish this at a competitive cost. This supported Henry Ford's basic philosophy that if you made the best product, only limited advertising and promotion would be necessary. Furthermore, it supported his philosophy that profit must and inevitably will come as a reward for durable products, excellent service, and good customer relations.

Mr. Ford wanted the Model A to be the finest automobile produced at low cost. This philosophy was impressed upon me by the adoption of forgings in place of malleable iron parts used in the Model T. Chevrolet used sheet-metal stampings, for many parts, and Ford used more costly forgings. Only luxury cars were equipped with hydraulic shock absorbers such as those adopted for the Model A; Chevrolet and Plymouth did not provide shock absorbers. Chevrolet and Plymouth were equipped with two-wheel brakes, as compared to the Model A having four-wheel brakes. For the Model A, wire spoke wheels were adopted from the more expensive luxury cars, as compared to stamped wheels used by the major low-cost competitors. Stainless steel hubcaps and grille coverings were used on the Model A in place of the cheaper chrome-plated stampings. Safety glass was adopted on the Model A at additional cost. Obviously, Mr. Ford was not influenced by his competitors' practices of using less costly designs. However, the competitors cleverly took their design savings and applied them to areas that could be seen by customers. The competitive marketing activities recognized the feminine appeal of ornamentation such as flower vases and visual appointments, and they incorporated these items in the interiors of car bodies. The competition also offered ash trays, but Ford Motor

Company could not furnish this feature because of Henry Ford's no-smoking policy. Mr. Ford's philosophy of providing outstanding functional features and the best of materials available in a low-cost car made the Model A an outstanding replacement for the Model T.

The Ford Model A coupe, 1928–1929.

The Model A, with its better brakes than those of Chevrolet, was always a delight for me. I took great pleasure in driving in front of a Chevrolet owner and stopping quickly. The cars would come together with a loud bang. Because the bumpers were spring steel and because suspensions were rather stiff, no damage occurred. Only the embarrassment of the Chevrolet owner was a concern.

As a result of Edsel Ford's quiet salesmanship with his father, in pleading the need for a more modern car, the long-overdue Model A was developed. The market anticipation was so great that more than 10 million potential customers appeared at the introductions of the Model A.

Henry Ford (left) and Edsel Ford (right), standing beside a Ford 1928–1929 Model A.

With the popularity of the Model A, competitive activity increased. Chevrolet replaced its four-cylinder engine with an in-line six-cylinder engine and a much more deluxe car body. Chrysler Plymouth adopted improved engine vibration control of its four-cylinder model. This brought pressure on the Ford Marketing and Engineering groups to meet this competition. Various engine designs were produced, including the Model B large-displacement four-cylinder engine with better engine mounting. An experimental five-cylinder, a V6, and several other concepts were produced and tested. Engine engineers did not have the knowledge of how to balance a five-cylinder engine or the V6 such as exists today. Therefore, these designs were built, tested, and discarded. Because Mr. Ford recognized that certain luxury cars of the 1930s had V8 engines, he said we should design a V8 to compete with the Chevrolet six-cylinder model.

As was typical with Mr. Ford, he assigned the engine project to several engineers to develop proposals. For security reasons, Mr. Ford finally took Ray Laird and two engineers to Florida with him and worked out the V8. His challenge to the engineers was that the engine block should be a one-piece casting. The Cadillac and Lincoln of that period had V engines requiring weldments because foundry practice could not produce a one-piece casting. No one questioned Mr. Ford's judgment, and the first experimental castings were scrap. Charles Sorensen, being a foundry man by early trade, did not dare tell Mr. Ford we were having difficulty. Thus, Sorensen kept it quiet for several weeks. After much experimental work, welch plugs or freeze plugs were introduced to port out the gases during the casting process. This permitted the casting to fill without voids. This was an industry first in the production of a one-piece V8 engine block.

The introduction of the V8 high-performance engine in 1932 by Ford set a new standard for performance in a low-priced car. The new downdraft two-barrel carburetor and manifolding were perfected with the help of suppliers. Customer satisfaction was expressed in the ability of the engine to start under extreme conditions and to outperform other road vehicles. In fact, John Dillinger, the highly recognized bank robber, wrote the following note to Henry Ford to thank him for such a great get-away vehicle.

> Hello old pal—arrived here at 10 a.m. today. Would like to drop in and see you. You have a wonderful car. Been driving it for three weeks. It's a treat to drive one. Your slogan should be, Drive a Ford and watch the other cars fall behind you. I can make any other car take a Ford's dust. Bye-bye, John Dillinger.

With the new engine and the cross-spring tight suspension, the Ford car was a favorite for racing during the 1930s and 1940s. The high performance of the first V8 resulted in Edsel Ford being selected to drive the Ford V8 as the pace car in the Indianapolis 500 Speedway. The production 85-horsepower V8 car had a top speed of 85 miles per hour, whereas other competitors' cars had a top speed of only 60 miles per hour. Pace car requirements at that time demanded a 100-mile-per-hour speed to remain ahead of the racers. We had to make sufficient changes to the V8 engine and axle ratios to meet the pace car requirements.

Henry Ford took a direct interest in the design of products and preferred to see things full size, vertical, and in front of him. He could stand back and view the parts or the full-size car at a distance, and he was great at proportioning and obtaining balance. We usually followed the practice of using colored pastel crayons for certain complicated assemblies or to accent certain areas of interest. Mr. Ford had difficulty in grasping complicated assemblies, and coloring permitted him to distinguish a piston or cylinder block of particular interest to him. He could read blueprints but was uncomfortable with complex drawings. At times, he would sit and direct the designer. You might be working on a cylinder block or transmission case, and Mr. Ford would say, "Well, now, that's too big. Take a quarter-inch off of that area," or "That part looks too heavy. Reduce the wall thickness to the minimum the foundry can cast." He was always very concerned about added weight. Today's excellent tools of design analysis and stress measurement equipment, plus computers, did not exist in the early 1930s. Therefore, much judgment and "eyeballing" for proper proportions was the name of the game.

One day, one of my transmission housings broke, and I was truly embarrassed. However, Mr. Ford told me that "If a part didn't fail in test, we would never know where metal should be added." I accepted his constructive criticism and felt he was "my kind of guy."

Mr. Ford's persistent overseeing of the Manufacturing and Engineering operations resulted in continuous challenges for the two groups. For instance, one day Mr. Ford came to my boss, Larry Sheldrick, tagging along the head metallurgist Hud McCarroll. In his hand, Mr. Ford held a piece of scrap fender stock from the body plant. He said, "We can make use of this by forming it into a cylinder for sleeving the engine block." Mr. Ford believed a hardened sleeve of steel would never wear out, as would the softer iron in the typical cast cylinder block. No one questioned Mr. Ford's reasoning, and hardened nitrated sleeves were developed and used in the engines—until we discovered that they never wore out, but neither did the piston rings wear in to provide proper oil control. With the greatest of precision control, the idea was never successful and finally was discontinued.

The bank holiday in 1933 and the tremendous downsizing of Ford Motor Company created difficulty in finalizing the design of the 1933 car. As money became available, a few Product Engineering old-timers were reinstated. Insufficient staff remained to carry out Henry Ford's assignments from his daily visits and to prepare the 1933 car for production. As a result, several of us were moved temporarily to the Ford Rouge factory to work with manufacturing personnel to finalize the production specifications of the car. I well remember the factory department heads' urgent demands for drawings and specifications to cover what they were providing for production.

As the group increased in size at the Dearborn Product Engineering Laboratory, Lawrence Sheldrick and many of his staff were relocated to Gate #4 of the Ford Rouge factory. This placed the group next to the Manufacturing Engineering activity and production lines, thereby enhancing the decision-making process. Charles Sorensen, who was in charge of all Ford manufacturing and Mr. Ford's right-hand man, could more effectively execute Mr. Ford's instructions without Mr. Ford being underfoot. Although Sorensen had no title, in today's organizational structure he would have been considered chief executive officer.

Relocation of the small Product Engineering staff to the factory enabled Henry Ford to spend more time with the advanced idea group at Dearborn and to be less involved in the daily decision making. This mode of operation continued until Henry Ford's death. Product Engineering was reestablished at the Dearborn Engineering Laboratory with the reorganization by Henry Ford II in 1945.

Chapter 6

Farm Interests

Henry Ford owned thousands of acres of land associated with the production of raw material supply. He invested heavily in coal and lumber land, which was necessary for production of the automobile. Being a farmer at heart, Henry Ford's personal attention focused on the 26,000-plus acres of farmland he owned in and around the surrounding areas of Dearborn. These farming operations were under his direct supervision and his farm manager, Ray Dahlinger. Henry Ford would give his farm manager instructions about what should be planted, where to plant it, and when to plant it. He also would oversee the harvesting of the crops. Henry Ford was a great steward of the land, and he ensured that his properties were well fenced and maintained in pristine orderliness. Roads were well maintained in the communities adjacent to his land, and Henry Ford took great pride in ensuring that those communities had good schools. He was a liberal benefactor to the areas surrounding his properties.

During his many travels with Dahlinger to inspect farm properties, Henry Ford at times elected to become involved in situations that were reported to us as most interesting. For instance, on one rainy morning as Mr. Ford and Dahlinger drove in outer Dearborn, they noticed a young boy and his sister walking to school. They offered a ride to the children, and as usual Mr. Ford inquired about how the children liked school. He was informed that school had been much more enjoyable before their favorite teacher had left. Later, Mr. Ford found that the young lady had gone to the city school for a higher paying job and a better facility. He had this followed up and arranged to have the teacher returned at an increase in salary. He also helped fund an improved facility for the school.

Another incident occurred that did not receive much publicity because the Dearborn police were somewhat intimidated by the Ford Motor Company. This incident occurred in one of Mr. Ford's typical drives through the country-side, and it reflects his keen interest in helping distressed people on an individual basis. One day, Mr. Ford and Dahlinger came upon an attractive forlorn lady residing on the curb of her previous home. Upon inquiry by Mr. Ford, the woman pensively said she had been thrown out of the building and had no place to go with her furnishings. In his empathetic way, Mr. Ford arranged to have his organization put her up in one of the farmhouses in Dearborn. A few days later, the Dearborn police came to the Ford Engineering Laboratory. The police indicated to the front office that Mr. Ford had furnished residence to a lady of ill repute who had been evicted from her previous residence. This situation was resolved quickly and without publicity. She was assisted in finding a non-Ford owned residence.

In addition to his great interest in making farming communities more pros-perous and farm chores less burdensome, Henry Ford envisioned that more effective farm equipment would give farmers additional time to pursue other sources of income. He and a few engineers had designed the Fordson tractor during World War I. This unique, low-cost tractor was the highest volume tractor of the period because of function and low cost. Henry Ford then directed his attention toward how to make more effective use of the farmer's free time. He believed farmers should be given an opportunity for off-the-farm employment during the off-season of farming. As mentioned previously, Mr. Ford had purchased approximately 26,000 acres of farmland in and around Dearborn, much of which had streams for water power. He envisioned that a small factory could be built with its own power plant and could become a source of supply of products for the auto factory. Factories at Nankin-Mills, Northville, and many other locations were established to provide seasonal work. These units produced production tools such as drills, taps, and machine tools. Other larger units followed, such as Ypsilanti, and these were year-round contributors of car components such as shock absorbers. This program helped the outlying farm communities by provid-ing sources of off-farm income. Henry Ford's early vision about the impor-tance of keeping small farming communities viable by offering off-farm employment proved successful.

Nankin-Mills was one of Henry Ford's many cottage industries that provided seasonal or off-the-farm work for farmers. (From the Collection of Henry Ford Museum and Greenfield Village)

In my many visits to Japan during the 1970s, I observed that the Japanese have adopted the early philosophy of Henry Ford. In Japan, many cottage industries supply the major factories. The added benefits of cost savings and helping to preserve small farming communities are now recognized by many forward-thinking U.S. and Canadian manufacturers. More outsourcing is occurring in the United States, and it is now being recognized as an important economic development in Iowa. For instance, in my home state of Iowa and elsewhere, many small factories, each having a few hundred employees and fewer than ten nonproduction supervisors and technical support employees, are successfully producing automotive parts. With so few nonproduction employees and great work ethics, parts are produced at half the cost of those produced in cumbersome and complex large corporate facilities located in major cities.

Henry Ford envisioned this trend approximately 65 years ago, and it offers substantial opportunity for stabilizing farm communities. It also offers the benefits of high-quality products made by U.S. and Japanese workers who have excellent work ethics, such as those found in the typical Japanese factory. More importantly, I am enthused to observe how our small farming communities are being revitalized and how an increasing number of major manufacturers are taking advantage of this great resource.

Henry Ford's fame and interest in farmers and farming practices drew unlimited suggestions from many sources on new projects that he should pursue. For example, one day Mr. Ford came into the Product Engineering Laboratory and said he had visited with a man named Faulkner who had written a book titled *The Plowman's Folly*. The book emphasized that the turning plow of the day should be banished and the soil worked without turning it over. This would save energy and more importantly prevent erosion and runoff of the soil in rolling country. When this theory was brought to Mr. Ford's attention, his curiosity was aroused and he wanted to proceed with testing Faulkner's idea to see if it was worthwhile. Mr. Ford had his farm manager Dahlinger dispose of the moldboard plows and prepare the seed beds by discing and dragging. Unfortunately, this was before herbicides were available for weed control, and after the first season, the fields were overrun with weeds. This did not discourage Mr. Ford, but he agreed to return the bottom plow to operation. Today, with the advent of herbicides and the many studies on soil erosion, bottom plows have been almost eliminated in tillage practices, and greater stewardship of our vital soil resources is being practiced. Both Faulkner and Ford were ahead of their time.

Henry Ford was truly a steward of caring for the soil and a man of great concern for the welfare of the farmer. His personality blended well with the typical farmer's great love of nature and his pride of producing something to benefit humanity. Henry Ford recognized from his own prior farm experience the toil and manual labor involved in farming operations. He dedicated much of his free time and resources to improve the farmer's way of life. During my association with Mr. Ford, it was obvious to me that he felt much more comfortable chatting across the fence with a farmer than dressing up and being recognized for his accomplishments.

Chapter 7

Chemurgy

In the early 1930s, William J. Hale coined the term *chemurgy* to describe his research in the use of farm and forest products as sources of raw materials for chemical manufacturing. This movement preceded the development of plastics. During the 1920s, the only plastics available were products such as Bakelite. Developed by Leo Baekeland, this material was the first completely synthetic resin and was used for items such as tooth brushes, combs, phonograph records, and automotive parts. The only other commonly used plastic was celluloid, which was used for collars, dentures, carriage curtains, clock cases, and the first photographic film. Unfortunately, celluloid was hard to mold, and it caught fire easily. Because of its flammability, celluloid became a safety hazard.

During the late 1920s and early 1930s, the chemurgy movement interested Henry Ford because it fit his vision of trying to develop organic materials from farm products that industry might use in place of metals. He also was concerned about the use of farm surpluses. Henry Ford envisioned that the use of replenishable products, in place of the limited reserves of nonrenewable resources such as metals, would be a great boon to the farming community while preserving natural resources. Henry Ford had become acquainted with the work of George Washington Carver and Carver's efforts in developing by-products from the soybean and the peanut. Henry Ford admired Carver because both men were kindred spirits in their dedication to helping farmers. Henry Ford had Carver visit the Product Engineering Laboratory and discuss the possibilities of the soybean and its by-products. At Carver's request, Henry Ford built Carver a log cabin in the Greenfield Village for housing. To build this cabin, a different log was brought from each state to show the great contribution Carver had made to the welfare of the nation. Carver indicated this was the type of house in which he grew up, and he did not want fancy accommodations.

A recent photo of me standing in front of the George Washington Carver cottage at Greenfield Village. Every log in this log cabin was from a different state.

Although this book is not about Carver, I cannot help but give him credit for his enthusiasm and encouragement of Henry Ford's vision. As you may know, Carver was the first black graduate of Iowa State University. He rose from the ashes of slavery to the pinnacle of scientific studies involving plant life and the development of plant by-products. He believed, as did Henry Ford, that every weed had a purpose and that a weed was simply a plant growing where it was not intended. George Washington Carver, Thomas Edison, and Henry Ford shared one thing in common: their dedication to the betterment of man was not oriented toward profit.

Henry Ford and Thomas Edison both admired George Washington Carver and his work, and they offered Carver a high salary to join their activities. Carver declined because he believed his divine inspiration was to help the poor farmers of the South in developing better food crops so that they would not be so dependent on cotton production. In addition, Carver worked untiringly to help the poor laboring South in raising a greater variety of foodstuffs, thus overcoming malnutrition that resulted from a typical Southern diet of grits, greens, and salt pork.

Carver was a Botany Department head at Iowa State University. After meeting Booker T. Washington, who was the head of Tuskegee University and a dynamic orator, Carver felt challenged to help this struggling black college attain its vision. Thus, Carver left Iowa State University to help the small Tuskegee University. Much has been written about Carver's great successes and contributions to the welfare of the South. This brought him world renown, but similar to Ford and Edison, Carver's interest in monetary rewards was secondary. At his death, Carver had an estate of approximately $35,000. God will surely bless George Washington Carver for his unselfish dedication to his mission.

Henry Ford, George Washington Carver, Thomas Edison, and Luther Burbank were in the forefront of the great possibilities of the chemurgy movement. Henry Ford started the project by setting up a distilling process in Dearborn to experiment with vegetable crop conversion to fibers. He wanted to determine what crops would produce what types and quantities of fibers. Carloads of tomatoes were distilled, as well as other crops such as carrots and potatoes. After substantial unscientific experimentation (similar to the experiments of Edison with the light bulb), the soybean proved to offer the most promise for fiber and other uses.

Soybeans had been introduced in the United States in 1804 from China. Being a legume, the soybean provided a nitrogen-fixing pod. At that time in the early 1900s, the soybean crop in the United States was used primarily for organic fertilizer. That is, it was turned under and not harvested. This practice continued until artificial fertilizers were developed. Without Henry Ford's involvement in the chemurgy movement, it is unlikely that we would have made great strides in developing both the supply and applications of the soybean. Henry Ford's willingness to spend millions of dollars in experimental work, without recognizing the financial feasibility of the projects, attests to his strong desire to help the farm community and to preserve the limited nonrenewable materials.

During these experiments, Mr. Ford brought to the Product Engineering Laboratory a glass of what appeared to be milk. He asked us to taste it and to tell him what we thought it was. We agreed that it tasted like cow's milk but wondered what it really was. Mr. Ford said it was a soybean by-product. When we asked about the cost, Mr. Ford indicated that the contents of that one glass probably cost $10,000 to develop. We agreed this was not very commercial. However, with later development, the soybean was used for production of artificial whipping cream and was put on the market as Presto-Whip.

Prior to the days of plastics being derived from hydrocarbons, Henry Ford also recognized that organic fibers could replace the use of rubber and zinc castings for ornamentation in car bodies. Likewise, mohair, which was goat's hair, was the deluxe upholstery for car bodies. Henry Ford became very excited about the possibilities of soybean by-products. With his enthusiasm, he asked his farm manager to plant the major part of his 26,000 acres of farmland with soybeans. Henry Ford also loaned free seed to farmers to encourage them to grow this crop for future industry use. His vision was that if the farmer could provide replenishable crops for use in industry, natural resource depletion would be extended.

Henry Ford was so enthusiastic about the potential of this project that he had the cafeteria (located next to his executive dining room) feed us soybean bread, soy milk, soy bean soup, and soy additives such as we have today. Unfortunately, the soybeans of that period were rather rancid in taste, even if they were healthful. We did not complain but were pleased as the quality of the soybean improved. During the 1932–1933 period, Henry Ford is estimated to have spent approximately $1.225 million on soybean experiments involving 300 varieties of beans. This resulted in many improved varieties of soybeans.

Further developments brought about the use of soybean resins for car glove-compartment doors, horn buttons, gearshift knobs, and various car body ornamentation. Ford finally developed a complete car body shell from soybean resin. Mr. Ford called in the press and showed them how he could hit the car body with an axe without damaging the vehicle. Approximately 35 years later, certain car manufacturers demonstrated how they could pound on the plastic car bumper without damaging it. This proves Ford was quite visionary.

The soybean oils from processing were used successfully in car paint specification. However, the cost of soybean resins was quite high compared to the cost of steel. In 1940, Mr. Ford asked me to have the operator seat of the Ford tractor made from soybean resins instead of the typical 38-cent steel pan. A few months later, Mr. Ford asked about the success of the tractor seat. I commented that the seat was cooler in the summer and warmer in the winter, as Mr. Ford had predicted, but the cost was $1.50. Mr. Ford was not concerned about the cost. However, we finally had to tell him that our farm customers were loosing their tractor seats because rodents and livestock liked the taste of soybeans. This ended the use of the soybean for this application.

With the advent of plastics from hydrocarbons, the soybean prevailed for only a short time in car body use. However, soybean oil continued to be used in paint and in many other commercial applications. An important spin-off of this experimental program was the development of artificial whipping cream. With added publicity, the industry became excited about potential by-products from the soybean. Henry Ford deserves much of the credit for commercializing artificial whipping cream and the start of the great chemurgy movement. He was a pioneer in increasing interest in the development of by-products from renewable plant life and thus conserving critical nonrenewable materials.

As previously mentioned, mohair was the deluxe car upholstery of the early period before the introduction of synthetics. Henry Ford had Robert Boyer, a Trade School graduate, work on soybean experimentation in an attempt to provide a fiber to replace mohair upholstery. After much experimentation, the Cheney Mill in Manchester, Connecticut, produced cloth from soy fiber. This new cloth was spun, similar to rayon, from soy fiber and was shown at the 1939–1940 World's Fair. Cloth of 65-percent wool and 35-percent soy fiber was made into a suit for Henry Ford, and soy fiber was mixed with rabbit fur to produce a hat for him. This pleased Mr. Ford and was the subject of interesting conversation. Again, the cost of these products restricted their commercial use; however, from these visionary projects came greater interest by the chemical companies in developing synthetic materials for car upholstery.

Henry Ford is wearing his suit made of soy fiber. (From the Collection of Henry Ford Museum and Greenfield Village)

Henry Ford's dedicated interest in helping farmers, by promoting the development of soybean production and its many by-products, parallels the efforts of George Washington Carver in developing the peanut and the sweet potato. The soybean now constitutes a major part of farm income. Both men's mission was one of bettering the welfare of others without concern for profit for themselves.

Chapter 8

Edsel Ford

Although it could be difficult to guess Henry Ford's next move, his only child Edsel was predictable and certainly one of the finest personalities with whom to work. Edsel was a perfect gentleman in all respects. He was courteous, sensitive, and a good listener. He had all the characteristics necessary to amplify the achievements of his father, but he so respected his father's ability to make decisions that he seldom offered a deferring opinion in his father's presence. Although Edsel would side with us on many decisions, during his father's absence he still left it up to his father to make the final decision. When we wanted to push a new feature or program and we knew the senior Ford would not approve, we would approach Edsel and show him what we had in mind. Edsel would always compliment us and be pleased; however, most times, he would tell us to cover the feature until he could discuss it with his father. From experience and discussions with the elder Mr. Ford, we knew which projects he would not approve; therefore, we needed Edsel to help us obtain his father's approval.

A typical example was convincing the senior Ford that we should put hydraulic brakes on Ford products. At the time, most of Ford's competitors had hydraulic brakes, but Ford did not. Ford products had mechanical linkages to each wheel instead of brake lines filled with hydraulic fluid. Industry had recognized that hydraulic brakes permitted more uniform braking forces to each wheel and better vehicle direction control when stopping.

We obtained a Marmon car with hydraulic brakes and asked Mr. Ford, Sr. to drive it and see the advantage. Unfortunately, one of the brake lines sprung a leak, the brakes failed, and Mr. Ford almost ran over a gateman. From that time, he would only relate how unsafe fluids could be, compared to mechanical linkage. We were told absolutely to not raise the subject again, and Edsel could not convince his father to reconsider. Years later, as trucks became larger, with longer wheelbases and a greater demand for improved braking, the subject was again brought up by Edsel. Eventually, Edsel convinced his father that we had a design with minimum exposure to brake line damage.

This painting of Edsel Ford is on display at the Greenfield Village.

Another characteristic of the Ford car was its two-spring suspension. The elder Mr. Ford was also adamant about using two cross springs to suspend the car, rather than the popular four-spring suspensions. He believed that the cross-spring design offered advantages of less unsprung weight and better roll stability than the better-riding four-spring designs of the competition. We tried to impress Mr. Ford that highways were greatly improved and that product ride was becoming more important to customers. Having a design that would have advantages on off-the-road rough terrain was not considered a major plus. We had Mr. Ford ride in a Chevy with its four-spring suspension, and his only comment was, "It sways so much that I am getting seasick." Edsel thought the four-spring suspension was quite an improvement, but he could not convince his father that we should pursue the project. Many attempts were made to change the type of suspension of the car. This finally was accomplished when Edsel's son, Henry Ford II, reorganized the Product Engineering activity after his grandfather's death.

With the limited engineering staff during the elder Ford's regime, testing and evaluation of experimental vehicles was subjective. Usually, the new feature or product was presented to Edsel and his driver for first evaluation. With Edsel's approval, the product then would be shown to Henry Ford. The senior Ford would have his farm manager Dahlinger take him for a ride to test the product. When they returned, Dahlinger would say the idea was acceptable or "no damn good." Seldom could we discover what Dahlinger or Mr. Ford found unacceptable about the rejected proposal; in most cases, we did not care to ask.

Durability testing of vehicles usually was done on Ford's airport test track adjoining the Product Engineering Department, or by taking the vehicle on a cross-country run. Standardized test and evaluation, such as tests used today by major car manufacturers, was not practiced in the 1930s. However, customer feedback and acceptance were monitored carefully to assure that the product was performing to customer expectations. Complaints were evaluated quickly, and corrections were adopted by involving only those necessary to produce and distribute the parts. Safety Committee meetings and Finance staff involvement were not a consideration. Pleasing the customer and giving the customer full value was of utmost importance to Mr. Ford and was emphasized by Edsel as well.

Edsel had a real interest in having the company produce a higher-styled luxury car. His lifestyle and artistic personality preferred something more luxurious than a basic Ford car. However, his father always was driven in a standard black Ford model. The senior Ford had interest only in a high-production concept that would be cost effective for the average family. My association with the elder Mr. Ford and his lifestyle convinced me that he wanted to be categorized as one of the multitudes. He was against "putting on airs."

In his early attempts to design the more costly custom car, the senior Ford had worked on development of the original Cadillac car. This design was not a high-volume concept and thus was of little interest to him. At that time, Henry Leland headed the Cadillac Car Company, and he eventually took some of his staff and started the Lincoln Motor Company. The Lincoln product was a high-quality, hand-made luxury car with a limited market. In later years when the Lincoln Motor Company became financially troubled, Edsel convinced his father that it would add prestige to Ford if they were to acquire the Leland operation. This was done, and the new acquisition became Edsel's primary area of responsibility and interest. The Lincoln program permitted Edsel to have decision-making responsibilities in an area that held little interest to his father.

Custom car bodies interested Edsel, and he established a design group headed by a very young man named E.T. Gregory, who was only 27 years old but was experienced in boat design. His charge was to pursue new ideas being promoted by overseas and domestic designers, and he hired several teenage Ford Trade School graduates, such as John Najjar. Unfortunately, body engineering as we know it today, involving surface contour development and the resulting important surface highlights, was not practiced in the early automotive days. The form and shape of a car body had progressed from square corners to simple, rounded surfaces. The art of surface development was not taught in formal schools, and major car manufacturers were in the process of training a few draftsmen in this new skill. The few skilled surface development artisans available to the industry were reluctant to train others. Each craftsman had developed his own set of French curves (a series of shapes with varying curvatures or radii), reflecting the surface forms of the period. These curves were used to blend surfaces favorable to the artistic eye of body designers. Body builders of the period were jealous of their abilities, practices, and processes. There was no exchange among competitors in sharing knowledge, as happens at today's Society of Automotive Engineers meetings.

Since the artisans' skills had evolved from the period of hand-built wooden carriages to a machine age using sheet metal, great challenges and opportunities existed in the transition. Ford Motor Company's great transition occurred in the development of the Model A, and it accelerated during the mid-1930s under Edsel Ford's discerning eye for more attractive products.

Those skilled in the art of surface development were in great demand. Most were not loyal to their companies and continually moved to increase their incomes. This situation finally was resolved at Ford Motor Company by hiring an instructor to train in-house apprentices. Ford had brought in a body engineer named Ed Scott, with whom I had the pleasure of working in updating supplier body drawings from Briggs and Murray Corporations. Edsel Ford, Joe Galamb, and Lawrence Sheldrick decided Ford should obtain in-house capabilities to do its own body development. A man named Valencourt, who was skilled in the art of surface development, was added to the Ford staff. He established a training area in the air hangar building. This building previously was used to assemble the Ford Tri-motor airplane. Graduate apprentice draftsmen from the Ford Trade and Apprentice Schools were taught this new skill. From this early start, the company developed many experts skilled in the trade. This new capability encouraged designers to express greater flexibility in form. Concurrently, the steel industry was encouraged, particularly by Edsel Ford and E.T. Gregory, to develop materials with greater formability. The result was some rather unique designs. A car body design department finally was established by Edsel under Gregory's supervision. This small group was isolated at one end of the EEE Product Engineering Laboratory in an area where we danced to Lovett's ballroom orchestra.

Henry Ford thought the few designers in smocks were something from outer space, but he gave Edsel the program with little interference. It was obvious to me that Mr. Ford recognized his son's artistic sensitivities and ability, which he did not possess nor were they of interest to him. Edsel had a discerning eye for proportions and balance; however, his father's main objective was a world of envisioning ways to make mechanical devices serve mankind and to provide those devices at the least cost.

The original Lincoln design obtained from Leland was typical of its day. It had rounded corners and metal shapes that skilled craftsmen could hammer out by hand. This was typical of low-volume car bodies that could not justify the more costly steel forming dies. This method of forming by hand tools often resulted in the thinning of metal in certain areas. Such thinning resulted in the need for soldering or filling in surface defects and considerable time-consuming filing and hand-finishing.

During the mid-1930s, Lincoln automobiles were considered among the best-crafted and prestigious luxury cars in the world. Edsel had a distinct eye for style and balance, and he nurtured the body styling and detail appointments. The wealthy customer was given several body options for vehicles that cost up to ten times that of a Ford car. Besides the several standard Lincoln bodies, other leading coach makers such as Brunn, Dietrich, le Baron, Judkins, and Willoughby also were available to create custom car bodies. The Lincoln chassis still was of a construction similar to the regular Ford; however, the unit was powered by a V12 engine that was remarkably smooth.

Many pacesetting Lincolns followed the prestigious early models having production and custom bodies. The sporty classic Lincoln Zephyr was introduced in 1937 as a result of Edsel organizing a small group of engineers and moving them to the Lincoln factory, thus removing them from the direct supervision of his father. Prior to this, Edsel Ford and Charles Sorensen prevailed on Henry Ford to move a major portion of the Product Engineering to the Rouge factory to facilitate decision making. Sorensen's office and the Manufacturing Engineering staff were located at the factory at the main entrance called Gate #4. This permitted Engineering and Manufacturing Departments to make decisions by personal contact, without time-consuming travel.

The 1936 Lincoln Zephyr.

Locating the two groups together at the Rouge factory also was necessary to prevent indecision on the part of Mr. Ford regarding every detail of change. Although the total engineering group numbered fewer than 50, a small number remained at Dearborn, Mr. Ford's headquarters, as a buffer group to handle his day-to-day new projects of interest. This small creative group did develop important design concepts which would be analyzed and adopted by the group at the Rouge factory.

Edsel Ford's office was located at the main administration building adjoining the Rouge factory, thus making this organization change important to those developing and producing Ford cars and trucks. Unfortunately, the office of Harry Bennett, the nemesis of the Ford management, was located in the basement of the administration building below Edsel's activity. Bennett was in charge of personnel and factory security. He would keep close contact with what went on in all operations and then would report back to the senior Ford.

Edsel Ford's office was located in the administration building adjoining the Rouge factory.

With more day-to-day decisions being made at the Rouge facility, Mr. Ford's direct contact with the major management team consisted of daily lunches at the Dearborn Engineering Laboratory. This enabled him to keep abreast of what was happening at the factory. Bennett provided information to Mr. Ford regarding detail changes occurring within the factory operations, which could be used for discussion at the lunch period. When Bennett could find items of which the key managers were not aware, this would strengthen Bennett's importance in the eyes of Mr. Ford. It was obvious to most of us that Bennett was trying to convince Mr. Ford that Bennett was the best source of information about what was occurring at the Rouge factory.

The elder Mr. Ford felt comfortable working with the small staff of engineers that remained at the Dearborn Engineering Laboratory. This permitted him to continue his daily suggestions of new projects. However, he still wanted to micromanage the daily operations of the entire organization. His lunches at the Dearborn Engineering Laboratory, with only a handful of his executives, assured him that each of his major staff knew in detail what was occurring daily in his own area of responsibility.

Harry Bennett's several-thousand security men were stationed throughout the Rouge factory, similar to spies, with authority from Bennett to judge how hard the men were working. They also gave feedback to Bennett that he could use to assure Mr. Ford that he knew what was going on in the corporation. Bennett used this to his advantage and to the disadvantage of those he wanted to blackball. He also used this practice to terrorize management and to mesmerize the senior Mr. Ford.

Mr. Ford would gather his few managers at lunch each day and quiz them about what had occurred since the previous lunch period. He would obtain input from Bennett's men that certain changes had been made on the car components, or that a certain piece of machinery such as a lathe or mill had been moved from one building to another.

During the lunch period when Mr. Ford asked Charles Sorensen, his world-wide manufacturing manager, about the movement of a certain machine in the Rouge plant (1,200 acres of machine tools), Sorensen would have to know the answer. When Mr. Ford asked my boss, Larry Sheldrick, about a certain change that was made on the car, my boss would have to know the details.

The EEE Product Engineering Laboratory executive dining room adjoined the employees' lunchroom. Henry Ford ate lunch here every day with his management team.

We prepared our supervisor for the daily luncheon quiz by the following process: Each morning before lunch, our small staff of engineers would go to Sheldrick and tell him in detail about all of the changes we had made on the product since the previous lunch period. Sorensen's manufacturing staff followed the same practice. With limited paperwork, this procedure worked quite well, and Sorensen and Sheldrick usually had the answers. However, as Mr. Ford's health declined, Bennett increased his pressure on Mr. Ford to convince him that Bennett was the only one who had all the answers and could be trusted. It was rather obvious to Sheldrick and Sorensen that Bennett was discrediting in the eyes of Mr. Ford the most loyal managers in the company. By so doing, the senior Ford would lose confidence in his managers, and thus Bennett's importance would increase. Bennett continued to obtain approval to have fired key employees loyal to Sorensen and Edsel Ford by discrediting those employees. This resulted in Sheldrick and Sorensen and other key executives leaving the company after the death of their champion, Edsel Ford.

Edsel Ford recognized the increasing negative influence Bennett was imposing on his father, and it caused Edsel to have severe anxiety and health problems. He also knew that Bennett had a stranglehold on the company through control of the payroll, transportation, communications, and factory security. All activities of the executives, including Edsel's activities, were monitored, and individuals could be set up for discredit by Bennett. Certain telephone operators monitored personal conversations of the executives and reported these to Bennett and his henchmen. Because of the frail health of the senior Mr. Ford, it became obvious to most of us that Bennett had almost convinced Mr. Ford to believe he could not trust his loyal management, including his own son Edsel.

As Henry Ford became more withdrawn, we had greater difficulty in communicating with him. Harsh treatment of the staff and labor was not typical of either Henry or Edsel Ford, but it was not countermanded by Sorensen because many of his staff now were under the influence of Bennett. However, Edsel and Sorensen continued to exercise management under an extremely difficult situation. This caused me and other managers of the company great pain to observe that Mr. Ford in his latter years was exposed to a person such as Bennett and the great damage Bennett could do in misleading him.

Having moved with my boss, Larry Sheldrick, and a small group to the Rouge factory at Gate #4, I could observe firsthand what was happening at the factory. Being responsible for the production design of car transmissions, rear axles, and miscellaneous other components during the late 1930s, I visited the manufacturing facilities almost daily. Working with the different factory managers of various buildings, I soon realized how effectively they ran their operations. In each major operation, the factory manager had only an office and a clerk. The clerk was there to determine at all times where the manager was located. Inasmuch as the total factory was a just-in-time operation with limited inventory, production stoppage could occur if a machine went down. This type of operation required the factory manager to be on the floor most of the day instead of sitting in an office.

Fortunately, Ford Motor Company had many major suppliers developing new concepts and playing a major role in updating products. Most often, these suppliers were a second source of parts supply to prevent downtime of the factory if one of the operations had emergencies. With the excellent suppliers' input, the company could also maintain a very small Product Engineering staff. Many of those supplier staff members were involved in research and development of new product ideas. Even with this extra help by suppliers, it was necessary for each Ford project engineer to do design and have experimental parts produced, tested, and put into production. This was accomplished with a rather limited number of personnel. My travels throughout the factory quickly convinced me that although Sorensen was in charge of the total operations, Bennett's men spied on the workers and supervisors. If Bennett's men did not like a production worker, they could haul him out of the factory without informing the supervisor of their actions. This created tremendous fear on the part of workers and resulted in their extreme insecurity. It also was obvious to me, having worked directly with Mr. Ford and Edsel, that this mistreatment of workers would not have been approved by either of the Fords. The elder Ford never fired anyone without good reason. Unfortunately, Bennett could set up many individuals, including Larry Sheldrick, and then squeal to Mr. Ford to get them into serious trouble. Bennett then would obtain Mr. Ford's approval to fire the person. Edsel being a real team builder with Sorensen and Sheldrick, the three made every effort to prevent separation of their team members. However, Edsel continually was distressed by Bennett's relationship with his father and his conspiracy to further his own position in the management of the company.

Much has been printed about the harshness of Henry Ford, but my direct experience with him convinced me that he was being misled by Bennett. In most cases, Sorensen could not counter the underhanded activities of Bennett and his henchmen.

Henry Ford's weakness was his inability to discuss the pros and cons of an issue, thus making it difficult to arrive at a compromise satisfactory to all parties involved. His temperament was such that he would quickly draw a conclusion without discussion. This characteristic was not typical of Edsel, but it did appear in Henry Ford II after many years of listening to others discuss at length their propositions that obviously supported their personal biases and conclusions. The impatience of the two Henry Fords seems to reflect their disgust resulting from others trying to lead them against their conceived better judgment. As time passed, the senior Ford seemed to withdraw from open discussion. Unfortunately, he spent too much time listening to Bennett.

Bennett's mistreatment of workers at the large Rouge factory led to a need of organized representation of the workers. Walter Reuther (later president of the United Auto Workers) was a tool and die maker in the Rouge factory major toolroom at this time. He was a capable organizer and spokesman for the workers, and he helped to organize them. Our Product Engineering group was located at Gate #4 of the Rouge factory. On May 26, 1937, we could observe the great disturbance when Walter Reuther, his brother, and a few others confidently walked across the 14-foot overpass bridge, from the parking lot to the factory, to distribute union circulars to the workers as they left the factory. Bennett had his toughest men meet Reuther and his men on the bridge. These Ford men were professional hit men on the factory security staff. They proceeded to pull the coats over the heads of Reuther's cohorts and beat them

Walter Reuther and two other U.A.W. organizers battle with Harry Bennett's security men at Gate #4 of the Rouge factory in May 1937. (From the Collection of Henry Ford Museum and Greenfield Village)

severely. This terrible mistreatment of Reuther was typical of Bennett's approach to negotiations. Reuther's attempt to bring dignified representation to the workers was unsuccessful at that time. Had it not been for Bennett's mistreatment of the workers, I doubt that the union would have prevailed. Henry Ford always paid the best wages in the industry, and the workers had no grievance except the way they were treated by Bennett's spies. Many of Bennett's men were paroled prisoners and underworld characters. Bennett prided himself in associating with such tough characters. He impressed Mr. Ford that this was necessary for security of the Ford family and company because Bennett had many underworld informers.

Mr. Ford's appreciation of workers and their welfare was obvious to most of us working with him. We also recognized that he had many characteristics and sensitivities that caused him to have difficulty in sharing who he really was. Inwardly, the elder Mr. Ford probably wanted to be the tough decision maker and to train Edsel to be the kind of a leader that could stand up to the pressures of others. Although both father and son had great love for each other, their chemistries were different and their interests quite dissimilar. Most of us saw that Mr. Ford's efforts to toughen Edsel by countermanding his decisions caused great distress to Edsel, which also affected his physical well-being. Although Edsel admired his father's ability to make decisions, he was prudent enough to recognize that more efficient management controls were necessary to ensure the future success of the company. When Edsel obtained advice from people other than his father, the elder Ford seemed to feel that Edsel was being misled. My association with both Fords gave me the impression that neither possessed the characteristics of being mean-spirited. Both Ford men marveled at the toughness of Charles Sorensen and Harry Bennett to stand up to others, but both were ill-equipped to display these characteristics, even if they may have been justified at times. The tough but fair management style of Sorensen was typical of the early factory supervisors of the day, and Mr. Ford was convinced that this style of management was acceptable. Unfortunately, Bennett's factory security personnel imposed unusually harsh control of the workers without proper supervision from Sorensen or objection from the elder Ford.

Bennett originally was hired as a security guard for the Ford family. Over time, as he developed his many organized-crime contacts and through his hiring of paroled prisoners as factory security guards, Bennett created situations to convince Henry Ford that Bennett could handle unusual situations. His "cops and robbers" lifestyle had a certain appeal to the elder Ford. As time passed, Henry Ford spent more time with Bennett, thus coming under his influence in judging the capabilities of management. This permitted Bennett to discredit those he could not intimidate. Quite often when Bennett would obtain Mr. Ford's approval to remove an executive, Sorensen and Edsel would try to intervene because these individuals usually were part of their loyal team.

An erosion of the Charles Sorensen–Edsel Ford management team further strengthened Bennett and his objective to prove to Henry Ford that Bennett was the only one who had all the answers. Because Mr. Ford wanted to micromanage the company, he was receptive to Bennett as a source of information about the detailed operations of his managers, including Edsel.

Bennett's espionage system permitted him to use information that would confuse Mr. Ford regarding whom he could trust. This created more conflict of emotions between Mr. Ford and his loyal managers and resulted in Mr. Ford's greater withdrawal from wise decision making.

Although Mr. Ford believed in paying high wages to his workers, he also believed they should return a good day's work. He provided them the necessary tools and resources to produce effectively. The conveyor system set the timing of each workstation and provided the media great delight in showing how fast workers had to operate. Recently, I viewed on public television a biographical documentary about Ford and his so-called "Tin-Lizzie." The exaggeration in the film of the speed of the workforce is probably why Mr. Ford said that "History is bunk." This was a good example of what the media can accomplish through warping the facts. It has been my observation over the years that, with every great positive development, negative press usually follows to attract greater media interest. Unfortunately, this occurred when Mr. Ford developed the moving assembly line in place of the previous stationary assembly of the automobile. Prior to the moving line, workers assembled the car similar to the average mechanic working on repair of cars. Mr. Ford's keen desire to find methods to reduce the cost of the car resulted in the moving assembly line, whereby each worker added his part to the final product as it passed his workstation. This resulted in going from limited assembly of 25 cars per day to assembling several hundred cars per day, thus offering substantial cost reduction and improved quality. Each worker did repetitive assembly and thereby became an expert in his particular operation. This also permitted the timing of the assembly process to ensure that each worker had reasonable time to perform his operation. This great advance in process was the subject of Hollywood interest and resulted in a movie depicting the workers working at an extremely hurried pace. The speed of the movie film then was increased to show the negative effect this advance in efficiency had upon workers.

This assembly line produced the Ford Model T at the Highland Park factory.

It is noteworthy that the positive results of the assembly line were passed on to workers and consumers. Henry Ford passed the savings to the customer and doubled workers' pay compared to the average public pay scale. This permitted Ford workers to put aside their bicycles and buy cars. The public benefited from Henry Ford's basic philosophy of providing a product that would more than justify its cost. This advance raised the standard of living of all industry workers and brought the ability of the average worker to have better transportation and a better lifestyle. Having been part of these early advances for greater efficiency, it is obvious to me that the benefits were downplayed by an overzealous media. Unfortunately, the image of the supposedly overstressed workers remains a historical document. Workers of that day did not feel mistreated, and Ford Motor Company was swamped with applicants for employment. As with all successful enterprises, there comes a time when the basic philosophies of the visionary become diminished by others who have ulterior motives.

Edsel's keen interest in developing a car of greater prestige resulted in the introduction of the Lincoln Zephyr, which was a concept car with a unitized body that had been developed jointly with Briggs body company. A short time later, this was followed by the introduction in 1939 of the Mercury to compete with mid-range cars such as Pontiac and Dodge. By this time, the Product Engineering group at the Rouge factory location had increased to approximately 75. This number included design and development personnel. Edsel also had a small engineering group under the supervision of Jack Wharam working on development of the Lincoln and Mercury at the Lincoln factory.

Test facilities were limited at the Dearborn Product Engineering Laboratory because Mr. Ford was using much of the shop to work on reconstructing antiques for Greenfield Village. In the 1930s, cold starting and heater tests were run in an outside environment in northern Wisconsin. At times, we would contract to use the Graham Paige car tunnel at its factory near Dearborn. Finally in 1939, Ford built a wind tunnel at Dearborn and converted the airport to a test track. Previously, experimental cars were run on public highways. To add greater capacity for testing components, the Product Engineering group at the Rouge factory established a small engine, transmission, and axle test activity in an old powerhouse to supplement testing at the Dearborn Laboratory. This facility also was used for assembling experimental cars. Here, the two Ford brothers, Henry II and Benson, were assigned to help assemble and test experimental models during their training period.

Two Briggs Manufacturing designs for the Lincoln Zephyr.

For a short time in 1940, the two young Ford men were assigned to Larry Williams (a black engineer) who headed the dynamometer tests. Bennett learned of this and tried to have Sheldrick, who was in charge of product engineering, reassign them. The two young men were pleased with their work assignments, and Sheldrick had Edsel's blessing to ensure that they were trained properly. Sheldrick and Sorensen prevailed over Bennett and had the blessing of the senior Ford.

Both Edsel and the elder Henry Ford believed in equal opportunity for blacks. Their policy of avoiding racial discrimination was ahead of its time. They never played race favorites; rather, they wanted to provide opportunities for all workers to help themselves. As a result, the Fords were considered great benefactors of the blacks. This resulted in many of the faithful blacks, who were working in the factory, resisting unionization. When the union strikers and lockout at Ford Motor Company occurred in 1937, the blacks remained in the factory because they feared union pressure as a result of their support of Ford objectives. This was a hazardous time for me. I remained in the Engineering Department overnight to protect the experimental drawings from damage, while the black workers were sleeping on the drawing boards.

The black workers feared the union members at the factory gate. To protect themselves in case of attack, these workers had sharpened blades of steel similar to swords. They spent several nights in the factory, and food was brought to them by the Rouge River boat slip within the factory. I well remember we had a young black within our engineering activity, and he was very anxious to go home. Because I parked inside the factory, I hid the young man in my car trunk. Then, as I hauled him through the motley and angry union crowd, I silently prayed that union pickets would not open the car trunk. Fortunately, I successfully smuggled the young man to Michigan Avenue and gave him his freedom. I then went home and took a shower, changed clothes, and returned to the Rouge plant to continue my vigil. When approaching the gate, a large and rather angry gathering stopped me and asked where I was going. As a young man with tough factory training, I asked them to get out of my way or someone was going to get run over. This resulted in ten men picking up my car and turning it around completely. They informed me in no uncertain terms that I should not try to pass through the picket line. This convinced me that unions also could be as tough as Bennett's henchmen.

Although Edsel, Sorensen, and Sheldrick continued to prevail upon the senior Mr. Ford that more nonproduction employees were needed to objectively make better decisions in the engineering, purchasing, and costing areas, their pleas fell on deaf ears. Mr. Ford would tell my boss Sheldrick that all that was necessary was to make a sketch on an envelope and then give it to Charles Sorensen, who would take care of it. That is what Henry Ford did in the early days of the Model T.

With inadequate staff and the lack of proper analysis before taking on projects, we often had to admit failure. For instance, in the late 1930s, the little Studebaker Champion was introduced and became a popular competitor to the Ford car. Mr. Ford came to Larry Sheldrick one day and suggested we develop a smaller version of the regular-size Ford to compete with Studebaker. We quickly developed a 60-horsepower version of the 85-horsepower V8 and proportionately scaled down the complete car. I worked on the transmission and rear axles.

Upon completing the product and tool design, Sorensen asked what the cost might be. A quick study showed that the small-version Ford would cost more than the full-size model Ford. The material costs savings were much less than the savings resulting from the high-volume full-size car having more efficient tooling. The small-car concept was dropped, and a quick decision was made to put the small engine in the full-size car as an option. This caused me concern because I had to change the transmission and axle ratios to provide acceptable performance. However, the car remained too heavy and underpowered, resulting in a limited market. Efforts were made to reduce the weight by welding stainless steel sheets in the side of the cylinder block in place of the cast walls. A lightweight aluminum transmission case was also considered. However, all efforts to reduce weight were not cost effective, limiting the life span of the model.

With continued encouragement from Edsel Ford, the engineering group at the Rouge plant became more aggressive in designing new car features. One project in which I was involved was moving the gearshift from the floor of the car to the steering column. Sheldrick had recognized that the gearshift and the hand brake in the floor were obstructions to passenger seating and comfort. As a young engineer, I vividly remember that the old stick shift in the floor usually ended up between the knees of one's girlfriend when in the drive position. Depending on how you looked at the situation, this may have been embarrassing. The design did permit one, when parked, to pick up on the stick and move it out of the way if desired. My design objective was to get rid of the stick shift for a cost not to exceed $1.75.

The size of the engineering group was so limited that each engineer had to do his own design and the testing of his design. A sample of my steering column design was produced and installed on my personal car. Having accomplished this, the floor was still obstructed by the hand brake. I proceeded to remove the hand brake because the car had reliable mechanical brakes instead of hydraulic brakes. It did not seem logical to have a backup mechanical hand brake for safety. In testing the shift device on a major highway in Detroit, I was stopped by a policeman because a taillight of my car was not working. Being "a bit too big for my breeches," I suggested that the officer should be writing tickets for speeders rather than for minor offenses such as taillight outage. The policeman called me a smart aleck and said he would have to drive me to the police station. In doing so, he said he had to drive. Imagine his surprise when he reached for the gearshift and the hand brake. I showed him how to shift the new design and explained that I had unbolted the hand brake and thrown it away. He wrote me a second ticket for having no hand brake on my vehicle.

Imagine my distress years later when my daughter Barbara bought her first car and my son Bob listed the options necessary and acceptable to the younger set. My $1.75 extra cost to put the control on the steering column seemed reasonable, but to pay an extra $175 to obtain the popular "four on the floor" option seemed extravagant.

With the adoption of hydraulic brakes on Ford trucks, Edsel (with our help) prevailed on his father that we could design a safe hydraulic brake system. This was accomplished in the late 1930s. Because the Ford still had only a two-spring suspension and a torque tube and radius rods to handle the over-turning forces of the one spring behind the rear axle, we were able to route the brake lines from the rear wheels forward without exposing them to brush and other hazards, such as was the case with typical four-spring suspensions. The front lines were equally secured from damage. The design proved to be acceptable and safe.

Edsel Ford continued to be a major force in supporting the Product Engineering objectives and in obtaining his father's approval through the late 1930s until his death in 1943. Edsel's interests centered on daily decision making to keep the corporation running. The senior Ford was more and more involved in his many interests unrelated to the automobile. One of Henry Ford's major concerns was the mechanization of the farm to improve the farmer's welfare. Thus, he spent considerable time visiting his extensive farm holdings in outlying areas around Dearborn, Michigan, and occasionally he visited our small group of engineers at the Rouge factory.

Chapter 9

Mr. Ford's Last Pet Project

With the Engineering Department move from Dearborn to the Rouge factory, we saw less of Henry Ford until we had a project that was of real interest to him. With the advent of more standardization of auto designs, the senior Mr. Ford lost much of his enthusiasm in the decision-making process. Mr. Ford was never a proponent of standardization because it was not his nature to be a follower. He was in his height of glory when the Model T differed in concept from all competitors' vehicles. However, his interest in farm operations never waned. In his youth, Henry Ford was interested in the large steam-engine-propelled threshing machines and sawmills. Later, he became firmly rooted in farming interests from his early years of working his first 40-acre farm. From personal experience, Henry Ford applied his ingenuity toward easing the hard work of farming. Furthermore, he had great empathy toward the financial success of the farmer.

Henry Ford always kept a small group of engineers at Dearborn to work on daily assignments, including sketches of concepts of new farm tractors. Two of his key concept engineers were Eugene Farkas and Karl Schultz. These two engineers continued sketching different concepts of farm tractors. Mr. Ford had Howard Simpson heading the Fordson tractor design updates. Although the Fordson introduction during World War I was a success, it never completely replaced animal power. In 1939, approximately 19 million animals were still being used for farming purposes. Henry Ford firmly believed that a concept tractor should be developed to replace the animals.

The Fordson tractor design was unique for its time because it was the first tractor to embody a unitized concept of engine, transmission, and rear axle forming the backbone of the vehicle and eliminating the frame such as that used by competitors. On other tractors, these components were bolted into a

Henry Ford and the 500,000th Fordson tractor produced.

framework, resulting in longer and more costly constructions. Although the Fordson tractor was continuously updated through the years, Henry Ford believed a better design was necessary to eliminate animal power. Various experimental tractors were proposed, including three-wheel offset to single-powered wheel concepts. However, none seemed practical. Finally, a new concept of mounting equipment on the tractor was brought to Sorensen's and Mr. Ford's attention by Eber Sherman, the national distributor for the Fordson tractor.

Harry Ferguson and his engineer, Willy Sands, in Ireland had been working on a concept of mounting the plow on the old Fordson instead of towing it behind the tractor, as was typical of all tractors of that period. The advantage of the proposed hitch concept would permit lifting the plow when it ran into an obstruction. It also would automatically adjust depth instead of using a gage wheel as furnished with the typical towed plow of that era. When the towed plow became lodged under a rock or tree root, the farmer had to unhitch the plow and often use a shovel to dislodge it. This problem was overcome with the proposed hydraulic lift and the three-point hitch. The Fordson tractor was being produced in the Ford Dagenham England factory. Thus, Ferguson and

Sands conveniently could work on their proposed design for the British Isles. Sands was a talented engineer and had worked out various mechanical lifts for the Fordson tractor.

Harry Ferguson had shown his hitch design proposal to Sorensen during one of Sorensen's visits to England. Sorensen wanted Ferguson to work for Ford to further develop the idea, but Ferguson was not receptive. Ferguson and Sands continued working on their hitch idea and finally convinced David Brown in England to produce a tractor incorporating Sands' development. The tractor was basically a 3/4-size scaled-down model of the Fordson design. Several hundred tractors were produced and sold in England and Scotland. These tractors had so many failures in the hydraulic mechanisms and structure controlling the hitch that farmers became frustrated and refused to purchase the concept, according to Harold Willey, Ferguson's field representative.

After Ferguson–Brown relations became strained, Ferguson had Eber Sherman approach Henry Ford to determine Ford's interest in the implement hitch idea. The contact was completed late in 1938, and arrangements were made to demonstrate the idea. A David Brown tractor was brought to Dearborn for demonstration for Henry Ford. Mr. Ford was perceptive enough to recognize the potential of the concept, even if it had been unsuccessful in England. In his usual way, Henry Ford quickly decided to proceed with the project, without consulting his management. Furthermore, because Henry Ford did not place any stock in written agreements and did not trust lawyers, he had a handshake agreement with Ferguson that Ford staff would design, develop, and produce the tractor, and that Ferguson would market it. Henry Ford asked Harry Ferguson to be a consultant to Ford engineers. Because the agreement between Henry Ford and Harry Ferguson was not in writing, Ford management were at Ferguson's mercy to interrupt the agreement. Later, this lack of a written agreement proved disastrous to Ford.

Sorensen and Sheldrick asked me to make sketches with Mr. Ford's Dearborn group regarding possible new concepts of tractors to incorporate the hitch design. Eugene Farkas, Karl Schultz, and Howard Simpson had been working for some time on different concepts of a utility tractor. I made several sketches, including a worm wheel drive, such as used on the old Fordson tractor. A Model R was mocked up and dropped for a construction that could use more car and truck components.

A December 1938 demonstration of the Ferguson tractor that had been unsuccessful in England. (From the Collection of Henry Ford Museum and Greenfield Village)

The project was of keen interest to Mr. Ford because he still had a burning desire to help farmers by eliminating animal power and the drudgery of caring for animals after a hard day's work. In his usual manner, Mr. Ford wanted a small group of engineers isolated for security reasons. A so-called "Blue Room" was established at the old powerhouse in the Rouge factory. This was typical when Mr. Ford wanted a project secured and permitted his personal attention. Sheldrick's engineering resources were more than stretched at the time, with the small number of personnel. Thus, Sheldrick asked that I be put in charge of the project. In selecting me, Sheldrick must have anticipated the difficulty that was going to occur, with the project headed by Mr. Ford and project managers Sorensen, Ferguson, and Sheldrick acting as backup to give me directions. I quickly found it difficult to obtain full agreement on details because the bosses appeared at different times. To keep peace and proceed with the job, I had to convince each of my bosses that he was in charge of the project. Their suggestions were of great help and, in most cases, did not conflict with each other or my own personal biases.

Henry Ford wanted to be involved in this tractor project. It seemed to have promise in fulfilling his dream of providing a classic design of product unique to the industry. Being involved in the daily decision-making process seemed to rekindle the enthusiasm of his early years, and his gentle piercing eyes sparkled with excitement. At this period of his life, Mr. Ford recognized that more cars were being standardized and that designs were in an evolutionary stage of the industry and were of less interest to him. With a new challenge, Mr. Ford reflected his old enthusiasm, and his gait seemed to increase. His interest in the project seemed to recapture and challenge him that he could make a major contribution. He was in constant contact to ensure that the project was moving at record speed.

This project is being covered in some detail now because it permitted me to spend a considerable amount of time with Mr. Ford and the top managers. It also gave me important insights about the strengths and the weaknesses of Mr. Ford's style of decision making. I sensed the tractor project duplicated his activity in developing the classic design of the Model T car. Time has proven that the N series classic tractor design concept introduced in 1939 has now been incorporated by industry in all tractors produced worldwide today. The importance of this tractor design to the farming community worldwide certainly has fulfilled Henry Ford's fondest dream. After 50 years, approximately 750,000

My demonstration model of the Ford–Ferguson tractor. (Submitted by Voyageur Press; taken from Robert N. Pripps' book, Vintage Ford Tractors.)

of these 9N, 2N, and 8N designs of tractors are estimated to remain in use today. It is also unusual that these units continue to sell at five times their original retail price. Unfortunately, Henry Ford did not live to realize the huge success of this project.

In his thoughtful and visionary way, Mr. Ford told our small group that the overall objective of the project was to replace animal power with machine power and to produce more foodstuff. This also was the original reason for production of the old Fordson tractor during World War I. Unfortunately, the Fordson tractor did not completely replace animal power in many farm operations. Mr. Ford indicated that the new tractor should have sufficient utility to perform all farm operations that required using animals. This would include all soil-working equipment, material handling, herding livestock, and fencing operations. We were to start with a clean sheet of paper and not consider what the rest of the industry was producing at that time. As a matter of interest, most other tractor manufacturers of that era were producing what they called "row-crop models." These units required high clearance for front cultivators and crop clearance. Because of their high clearance

Henry Ford (left) and Harry Ferguson (right) discuss my demonstration model of the Ford tractor with the Ferguson three-point hitch.

and a tricycle front axle for adapting front-mounted cultivators and mounting corn pickers, these tractors did not readily adapt to the many utility operations of farming. The various tractor manufacturers' designs had evolved in much standardization of design, and Mr. Ford strongly believed a new concept was overdue.

Mr. Ford said that to be successful and cost effective to farmers, the tractor should not cost more than the combined cost of a team of horses or mules, a set of harness, and the ten acres of land required to grow food for the animals. If the project was successful, this would eliminate the toilsome caring for animals after a hard day's work. Likewise, farmers could raise foodstuff from the ten acres of land rather than raising fodder for animals. If we could meet this objective, Mr. Ford was convinced he finally could accomplish for farmers what he did with the Model T car in providing a real value. A profit or return on investment was never mentioned in the discussions.

With these marching orders, Mr. Ford asked me to first measure a railroad boxcar. As usual, we never asked questions about why. When I returned, I was informed that we should have a design that would permit shipping 14 identical tractors in the boxcar to keep freight costs to a minimum. Other tractor manufacturers were making a variety of different sizes and styles of tractors and were forced to ship by rail on flatcars, at additional cost. Mr. Ford was always envisioning ways to keep costs to a minimum. It was obvious to me that Mr. Ford was remembering his basic concept of a low-cost car when he said, "You could have it any color you pleased—as long as it was black." It also reminded me that the engineers of the Model T days had told me Mr. Ford directed them to have the old Model T running boards made from lumber from the suppliers' crating. Therefore, Mr. Ford had the suppliers make crates with the appropriate size of material.

With feedback from a large consumer base, customers frequently suggested ways to improve and reduce cost. On one occasion, I remember the wire between the spark plug and the distributor failed on a farmer's car. The farmer took a corset stay (i.e., a flat spring wire) from his wife's intimate apparel and used it as a ready replacement for the wire. This idea appeared on the early Ford car as a cost savings. This example proves that Henry Ford listened to customer suggestions to make improved Ford products.

As with the old Model T car and its popularity, this principle later proved to be the case after many thousands of Ford Model 9N utility tractors were put into the hands of users. As users recognized the potential utility of the design, they devised various implements and equipment to enhance product usage. For instance, one farmer recognized the need for easy changing of tread widths for row crops, and he devised a jack system using the tractor's hydraulic lift that permitted the tractor to raise itself for adjusting all four wheels. Other innovators developed equipment such as loaders, scrapers, and cordwood saws to enhance the utility of the tractor.

Being the project manager, Mr. Ford gave us explicit orders that the tractor should be brought to production as soon as possible. There was no doubt in anyone's mind that his few key managers would make an all-out effort.

Although Ferguson provided a David Brown tractor similar to the old Fordson tractor, we decided that little of the concept could be used and still meet Mr. Ford's objectives of cost and utility. The arrangement and construction of components did not lend themselves to a low-cost manufacturing concept. Mr. Ford indicated that Ferguson was to be a consultant to the group. Sands, who had developed the hitch idea, would help us adapt the concept. In carrying out the project, we quickly discovered that Ferguson could not read blueprints effectively because he was a marketing man. Sands could interpret blueprints, and Ferguson had an assistant in John Chambers who looked over our shoulders as we developed the designs. Chambers became the liaison for Ferguson and Sands when they were not present. We also learned that Sands was the inventor of the hitch idea but that Ferguson had taken out the patent in Ferguson's name. This practice is legal in England but not in the United States.

In January 1939, nine other engineers joined me to quickly develop a concept that we believed would meet Mr. Ford's objectives. Because of time constraints and cost, we decided to use as many high-production components as possible from the current car and truck production, without compromising performance. This was accomplished by using components such as four cylinders from the high-production V8 engine, the car wheel bearings, the car clutch and electrical system, the truck axle gears, and truck brakes. This also would permit ready availability of service parts from Ford car dealers. The project seemed to put a sparkle in Mr. Ford's eyes as he again had an opportunity to express his innovative spirit and be a project engineer. With Mr. Ford's backing and no resistance from Sheldrick or Sorensen, we made great strides, without committee meetings or paperwork.

The tractor project was located at the Rouge factory, thus permitting all resources and disciplines to be readily available for daily consultation and action. Twice daily, the engineering drawings were copied and distributed to all factory functions for preparation of manufacturing. Because the product was all new with the exception of car and truck components, extensive tooling was required for low-cost production transfer lines.

The manufacturing group synchronized its activity with the engineers and in some cases finished the tooling before the detail drawings were completed. For instance, the pattern makers working on major castings, such as cylinder block, transmission, and axle housings, completed the patterns before the detailed sectioned views of the completed castings were finished. Machine tools and transfer line machinery were in process as the designs progressed.

We began our work in early January and completed a prototype by mid-April, which was then ready to evaluate for product performance. Because a special design of new rear wheels was not available from industry, a wooden form was produced and used to provide a cast wheel. Additionally, sheet metal dies were not available for the prototype; thus, hand-formed temporary metal was used for test purposes. Sufficient tests confirmed stability of design, and production commenced in July 1939, six months from inception. Although this detail may not interest many readers, it demonstrates what can be accomplished in six months instead of the typical three years for major project development of today. Obviously, the decision making involved top management and those experienced in the skills necessary to produce designs and tooling for efficient production.

With increasing demands on industry today to shorten development times, this particular project reflects the possibilities when you have an enthusiastic project leader such as Mr. Ford, who also had authority to make daily decisions without proliferal input from accountants and legal consultants. However, I must admit that having a better idea of actual project costs prior to production would have been helpful. With the urgency to fulfill Mr. Ford's time objective, estimated costs were rather rough. We knew the cost of the current parts being used, and we made quick estimates of the new parts. Obviously, our progress was not delayed by extensive cost analysis. Additionally, it is likely that with more legal counsel in drawing up the agreement between Henry Ford and Harry Ferguson, distress might have been eliminated when Ferguson later left with the Ford drawings to make his own tractor.

Today the young generation claims that new management has determined the effectiveness and need for establishing program groups comprising all disciplines necessary to develop the product. This has proven effective in shortening time schedules. I am impressed with some of the new terminology that has been coined to describe this process. I often ponder why it has taken industry leaders 50 years to return to the basics of less management and more empowerment of employees who have the necessary experience to make wise decisions. The old adage that "Decisions should made at the lowest possible level" should continue to be practiced.

The first tractor prototype was equipped with rubber tires instead of solid steel wheels, such as those of the British Fordson and the David Brown model. We quickly discovered that the hitch, with depth control, would not work because it sensed a stable depth of the implement and vehicle. As the rubber tires deflected, the hitch sensed a different load and the implement would porpoise. After considerable test with various soils, structures, and types of implements, the hydraulic system valving was modified to correct the problem. Other changes were made to the hitch system to make it satisfactory. For instance, the linchpins used on the Ferguson proposal would flip out, causing the implement to become detached. A new design of linchpin was developed, incorporating an over-center spring loading, which corrected the problem. Unfortunately, this item was never patented and has been standard on all tractors for the past 55 years.

It was agreed that Ferguson would be responsible for developing the necessary special three-point hitch implements as part of the new concept. Upon completion of the tractor prototype, we learned to our amazement that the only implements Ferguson had were those used in England. These were unacceptable for the North American farm market because soil conditions and farming practices in America differed from those in England. Ferguson had no engineering staff available to design implements. Unfortunately, we had a new tractor requiring new basic implements such as plows, cultivators, planters, and harrows compatible with the hitch attachment. Thus, our Ford engineers began designing basic implements. Our Ford engineers had no experience in designing farm implements because the implements for the old Fordson tractor had been furnished by outside manufacturers. We quickly purchased an Oliver plow used with the Fordson. No drawings were used by plow makers of the day, because blacksmiths used a master form to shape parts. We had the Ford body engineers develop surface drawings of the shape of the plow moldboard in order to mass-produce the part. We also determined that all plow beams of the day were made from rerolled railroad rails. This resulted in beams that were heavier than necessary to provide sufficient strength in the highest stress area. Ford engineer Oscar Molychevitch, who was an excellent mathematician, designed a cast steel plow beam with uniform stress throughout the complete beam. This was a first and resulted in lighter weight and less cost.

Ferguson indicated as a consultant that the moldboard of the plow and share should be sufficiently accurate in alignment to ensure that no joint line should be visible when assembled. We did not question his judgment; therefore, a

The 1939 9N tractor experimental prototype, developed in only six months.

special contour grinder was developed and used to accomplish this precision. Unfortunately, we did not realize that the level of perfection in the rest of the industry was substantially lower. The cultivator was made with similar precision. Ferguson was a consultant in detail that proved to be costly and, in many cases, unnecessary. However, giving him full credit, he did have genuine marketing savvy from the tractor operator's standpoint. For instance, Ferguson asked that all bolts used on the tractor and implements have rounded ends and not project beyond two threads of the fastener. This would prevent the operator from catching his or her clothing. All hardware had to be of alloy steel hardened and plated. Other implement manufacturers paid little attention to hardware lengths or finish. In keeping with Mr. Ford's philosophy of producing high quality, we did not question Ferguson's suggestions. Both Henry Ford and Harry Ferguson wanted one wrench to adjust both tractor and implements. A simple open-end wrench was designed, with measurement marks to permit the farmer to adjust implements and make tractor adjustments. This eliminated the operator carrying a large toolbox of wrenches to make field adjustments. Special hardened and plated bolts and nuts were provided to match the one wrench.

Upon completing the tractor design, many patentable items became apparent. Ford successfully proved that the Selden patent (i.e., the patent on the early automobile) was invalid and that patents offered little security from infringement. In the early years, the U.S. Patent Office spent only a few hours searching for prior art before issuing a patent. Mr. Ford believed patents had to be litigated in court, with many hours of research necessary to uncover prior art, before a patent was proven worthwhile. Because Harry Ferguson knew Henry Ford's position on patents, he asked Mr. Ford to permit him to take the new patent applications covering the Ford tractor under his name, as he had done with the Willy Sands' hitch invention. Mr. Ford directed our engineers to do so. When Ferguson and Ford separated, the question of the ownership of the design later proved embarrassing to Ford Motor Company.

Eber Sherman, the national distributor for the old Fordson tractor and the man who brought Harry Ferguson to Henry Ford's attention, became Ferguson's partner in establishing a distribution system called Ferguson–Sherman. Much of this arrangement was already in place within the Sherman activity. Because both had limited capital to invest and needed only a small staff, they were given space in the Rouge factory B building near the assembly of the tractor. Ford provided most of the invoice and shipping information. Ferguson–Sherman had only a small staff to handle marketing and service training responsibilities.

In establishing the retail cost of the tractor, Ferguson made every attempt to "butter up" Mr. Ford about Mr. Ford's reputation in producing products at low cost and his desire to produce a tractor that would meet the objective of eliminating animal power. Mr. Ford inquired from our group as to what was the lowest-cost tractor on the market at that time. We found that the little Allis-Chalmers Model B met this inquiry. This little tractor was a basic garden tractor with a hand crank and a simple drawbar. Mr. Ford told Sorenson and Sheldrick that Ford should compete with this Allis-Chalmers model. As usual, no one questioned Mr. Ford's judgment, and we still had no idea regarding the costs of the new 9N tractor. Mr. Ford was not concerned that the Ford tractor was highly styled, having additional features of self-starter, a three-point implement hitch with hydraulic depth control, fenders, and lights. Without input from

91

Ford management, Mr. Ford agreed to establish a retail price of $585 for the new tractor, which met the objective of the cost of a team of animals, the set of harness, and the cost of ten acres of land to feed the animals. This price also was competitive with the Allis-Chalmers Model B.

The Ford manufacturing challenge to produce the tractor at a price that included markups by distributors Ferguson–Sherman and dealers was not addressed initially, because we could not tell Mr. Ford the cost. The manufacturing operation was merged with the car production, which further confused the true cost of production. Mr. Ford's great objection to having nonproduction cost control employees, or paper shufflers as he called them, delayed information about the true cost of the tractor. However, if we would have had today's level of nonproduction financial support and the resulting overhead, it is questionable whether this important project would have been pursued.

The 1939 Allis-Chalmers Model B was a basic garden tractor.
(Submitted by Voyageur Press; taken from Robert N. Pripps' book,
Vintage Ford Tractors.)

In mid-June 1939, the Ford 9N model tractor was demonstrated successfully to the North American press, potential distributors, and guests. The demonstration plot was a one-acre fenced plot. First, horses were demonstrated in plowing the plot. The usual problems of horses becoming entangled in their harness when pulling the plow from an obstruction was impressive. A typical tractor with a drawn plow was an improvement; however, when the plow became hung up on a tree root, the operator had to unhitch and manually maneuver the plow and then hook it up to the tractor again. In addition, the trailed plow missed the corners of the field.

With some fanfare, the Ford tractor entered the plot and proceeded without problems. As the plow met unusual obstructions, the operator backed up and with a flick of the hydraulic control lever lifted the plow, moved over the obstruction, and dropped the plow back in the ground. Furthermore, with the implement hitch, the plot could be tilled and cultivated without the loss of corners. In addition, with the ability to raise the implement, the plot could be tilled without leaving tire tracks. To show ease of operation, a nine-year-old boy demonstrated how effortlessly the tractor and controls could be operated. This was believed an important objective because many farm chores now could be performed by the farmer's wife and children, under proper supervision. A number of tractors of that period required great physical effort to manually release the engine clutch and to control heavy implements.

From 1939 through the shutdown of industry for war production in 1941, the Model 9N Ford tractor concept gradually eliminated the doubts of the old-time farmers. The new tractor demonstrated well, and farmers soon observed that they could replace their old concept of heavy, high-clearance tractors with a compact and less expensive unit. Additionally, they could eliminate animal power and produce crops on the land formerly used to support the animals. Unfortunately, during the subsequent war period, a shortage of critical materials required reducing tractor production to only a few units. A Model 2N tractor was produced, which incorporated less rubber, copper, and other materials that were so important to war production. The Model 2N tractor was equipped with steel wheels, magneto, and aluminum radiators to eliminate critical war materials.

The first production of the 1939 9N tractor. (From the Collection of Henry Ford Museum and Greenfield Village)

The production of this classic design of tractor in 1939 fulfilled Mr. Ford's dream of providing a tractor that would replace animal power throughout the world. Sixty years later, the basic design concept has been adopted worldwide by the tractor industry for all sizes of farm tractors.

Chapter 10

Ford's War Effort

As the United States entered World War II, the U.S. Department of Defense (DOD) quickly recognized the lack of up-to-date weapons and equipment to support U.S. military forces. Henry Ford had little initial interest in turning over the Ford resources to help in the war effort. However, Edsel Ford and Charles Sorensen were involved with most of the decision making, and they prevailed upon Mr. Ford as to the necessity of helping in the war effort. Ford, General Motors, Chrysler, and all major manufacturers were solicited to assist in the design and development of new military equipment. Unfortunately, the DOD had reduced civilian engineering activity to a minimum during the prewar years. This left the DOD group with inadequate capability to update military equipment. Only through the help of the strong technical and manufacturing resources of U.S. industry did Europe and the United States finally survive the better-equipped German military forces. The total U.S. industry capability became the only salvation in equipping this nation for the all-out war effort.

Ford initially accepted several important projects. The Product Engineering staff at that time numbered only 75, and most of that staff were transferred to various war machine development. One of the first projects was the design and development of a reconnaissance vehicle. The Department of Defense initially had given the project to the Bantam Corporation. Because of the limited capability of Bantam and the urgency of the project, the project was reassigned to Ford and Willys-Overland to quickly design, develop, and build a prototype for performance evaluation. Ford designed and built the first prototype for approval and shipped it to the Department of Defense Halobird Proving Grounds in Maryland. This vehicle, later known as the Jeep, was approved after cross-country durability tests were completed successfully. Ford was given an order to build a production run. Ford's drawings then were submitted to the Department of Defense, and copies were transferred to Willys as a second source. It is interesting that Ford's drawing nomenclature on the drawings used a "GP" prefix for part numbers, which later was referred to as Jeep vehicle instead of the more lengthy Department of Defense name identification of Reconnaissance Vehicle. When the war concluded, Ford was anxious to return to car production and did not want to continue making vehicles for the War Department. However, Willys needed additional vehicles in its vehicle lineup for postwar production and continued the peacetime production of such vehicles.

Ford has the basic patents on the so-called Jeep (Patent Nos. 2,317,619, 2,317,620, and 2,319,869). The patents were issued to C.F. Kramer of Ford Body Engineering Department. Willys elected to trademark the name "Jeep" and has done well over the years in expanding the basic design of Ford. Much discussion exists regarding which company developed this rather unique vehicle, and history would lead you to believe that Willys and Chrysler should receive the credit. Note that subsequent to the war period, a hearing was held in the Federal Court, Detroit District, as Willys-Overland was charged by the Federal Trade Commission with misleading and false advertising wherein it claimed to have designed the U.S. Army 1/4-ton 4 × 4 Reconnaissance Truck GP (General Purpose). It was proved in the trial that Ford drawings were copied and used by Willys as a second source. The Federal Court issued a cease and desist order to the Willys-Overland Company from claiming to have designed this vehicle. It is remarkable how facts become recorded as time passes and simply proves Henry Ford's observation that much of history is bunk.

Although Henry Ford remained active in decision making, Edsel Ford and Charles Sorensen, cooperating with the Department of Defense, continued as a strong force in helping with other Ford war projects. They were requested to become involved in the production of the Rolls-Royce aircraft engine for England. Drawings were analyzed by the Product and Manufacturing Engineering activities for possible production by Ford. This review indicated that the design did not lend itself to mass-production, and thus Ford dropped the project. The project was picked up by the Packard Motor Company. However, Ford commenced the design of a V12 overhead dual-camshaft all-aluminum engine for a possible production replacement. This engine was never adopted for aircraft production but did have application for future military tanks.

Attachment 1. (b)

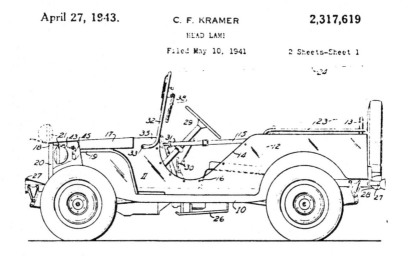

April 27, 1943.   C. F. KRAMER   2,317,619
                         HEAD LAMP
                    Filed May 10, 1941   2 Sheets-Sheet 1

FIG.1.

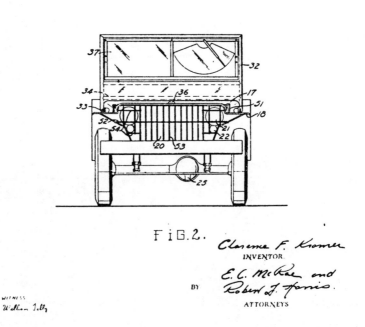

FIG.2.

Clarence F. Kramer
INVENTOR.

E. C. McRae and Robert J. Harris.

BY

ATTORNEYS

WITNESS
William Tilly

Patent drawing of the Ford GP reconnaissance vehicle, Patent No. 2,317,619 issued to Clarence Kramer of Ford Motor Company.

Attachment 1. (C)

April 27, 1943.   C. F. KRAMER   2,317,620
                              SEAT

                          Filed June 7, 1941

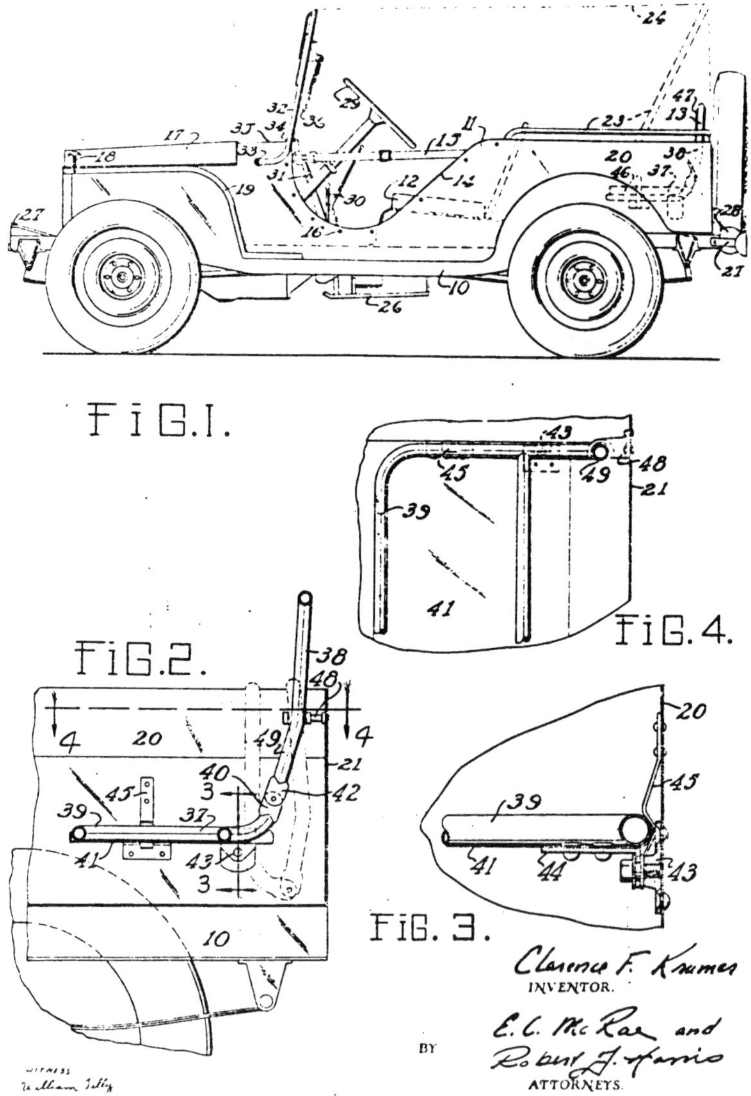

FIG.I.

FIG.2.

FIG.4.

FIG. 3.

Clarence F. Kramer
INVENTOR.

E. C. McRae and
Robert J. Harris
ATTORNEYS.

WITNESS
William Jolly

BY

*Patent drawing of the Ford GP reconnaissance vehicle, Patent
No. 2,317,620 issued to Clarence Kramer of Ford Motor Company.*

Attachment 1. (a)

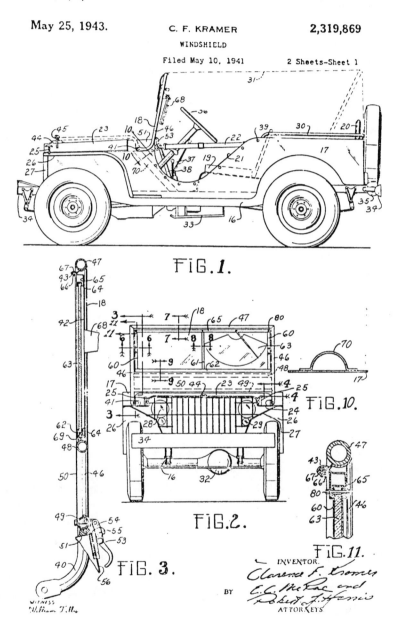

May 25, 1943.   C. F. KRAMER   2,319,869
                             WINDSHIELD
                    Filed May 10, 1941   2 Sheets-Sheet 1

FIG.1.

FIG.2.

FIG.3.

FIG.10.

FIG.11.

INVENTOR.
Clarence F. Kramer

BY

ATTORNEYS

WITNESS
William Tilly

Patent drawing of the Ford GP reconnaissance vehicle, Patent No. 2,319,869 issued to Clarence Kramer of Ford Motor Company.

The Ford GP reconnaissance prototype vehicle. The vehicle was submitted to the U.S. Department of Defense, tested at Halobird Proving Grounds in Maryland, and approved for production.

Edsel Ford and Charles Sorensen also were asked by the Department of Defense to furnish engineering help to the Aberdeen Proving Grounds in Maryland to redesign the current M3 medium-size tank. This vehicle had a shortcoming of inadequate fire power and very poor field performance in combat. It was no match for the German military tanks, and the U.S. tanks were being blown out of the field by the superior gunfire of the German army. With so few engineers on the Ford staff, Sheldrick believed I could be sacrificed with least disturbance. Because we had finished the Jeep design and my tractor design responsibilities were on hold, Sheldrick suggested that I take three young men with me and visit the Aberdeen Proving Grounds to offer my services.

The first thing that caught my attention at Aberdeen was that a gentleman named General Christmas was in charge. This seemed rather significant because it was the Christmas season. Of more interest to me was his daughter named Mary Christmas. I felt this was rather unique.

My little group was assigned to the department responsible for tank development. My marching orders were to redesign the front half of the M3 medium-size tank. Not having experience with tank operations, I had to determine the problems before developing a solution. I was told that the front track drive design, consisting of three large castings, was of a shape and construction susceptible to gunfire piercing the operator station and killing the driver. Furthermore, the three large carriers for internal drive mechanisms were made of armor plate that was difficult to machine.

After several weeks of study, I completed a construction that overcame the objections. The three large rather bulbous castings were replaced by a one-piece casting of armor plate requiring only limited machining. This permitted the front of the tank to be ballistically shaped to prevent armament piercing it and killing the operator. The drive mechanism was mounted on a one-piece carrier of easily machineable cast iron and permitted easy assembly in the large armor plate front casting. After receiving approval of the design from General Christmas and the Department of Defense, we were asked to have a sample produced to see if the concept would work. Inasmuch as the John Deere Waterloo Works in Iowa was one of the suppliers of the older design M3 tank transmission and axle, I was asked to go to Waterloo and have that company produce a sample of my new design. Little did I know that 20 years later, I would direct the John Deere Tractor Engineering activity at Waterloo.

With the urgency of the war effort, the nine manufacturers of the old M3 tank were asked to begin tooling the new design before a sample was produced. Although I recognized the urgent need for a new design, I was concerned that my concept may have problems. Fortunately, the design was structurally stable and fulfilled the requirement. Upon my return from my Aberdeen assignment, Sorensen was so pleased that he gave me a bonus for my effort. Before I could relax, Sorensen informed me that Ford also was going to be a supplier of the new M4 medium-size tank. He asked me to be the resident engineer to help Ford produce the tank at the Highland Park factory, where the old Model T car had been produced.

The Sherman tank assembly line at Ford Motor Company in 1942.

Although I had no responsibility for designing the rear half of the tank, I did have an opportunity to assist in developing various engine applications for the new model. The old M3 tank had a radial aircraft engine that was extremely underpowered. This tank would hardly pull a chicken from its nest, so to speak. Chrysler proposed putting five automobile engines in radial formation—a real service problem and not practical. General Motors offered a two-diesel-engine concept that had promise. Ford finally took advantage of its V12 aircraft engine design and produced a V8 version for the tank. Later, Ford provided the V12 design for an even larger tank than the M4 Sherman tank. The larger tank continued development after the war by the Department of Defense.

An all-out effort by industry convinced me that U.S. industry resources were the salvation of this nation's security. It was remarkable how quickly our industry responded in the hour of need and made up for the shortfall of experience in the Department of Defense.

The M4 Sherman tank and components, now on display at the John Deere Waterloo Works in Iowa.

During our daily travels from the Lord Baltimore Hotel to Aberdeen, Maryland, every morning, it was our pleasure to visit with my friend Ed Cole from General Motors, who also had a small group of engineers helping the Department of Defense in the design of a small tank. At that time, Ed Cole was chief engine engineer at the Cadillac Division of General Motors. Ed commuted in a Cadillac, but my guys rode with me in a black Ford. Chrysler also went all out in the production of tanks but concentrated its engineering on military trucks. Caterpillar sent several engineers to help make detail drawings of my designs.

From this experience, I hope and pray that our nation will maintain a strong technical capability in development and manufacturing to ensure the necessary resources to respond to future war threats. Care should be taken in outsourcing to other nations in order to avoid reducing our future basic capabilities.

A major project that consumed much of Edsel Ford's and Sorensen's time was the B24 Liberator bomber production. Much has been written about this project, and I was not directly involved because of other activities. Although the senior Mr. Ford was not enthusiastic about the project, Edsel Ford and Charles Sorensen prevailed upon him. Sorensen accepted the challenge, and, with his aggressiveness, he and his staff built the Willow Run factory in record time and did a remarkable job of tooling for high production of the important bomber. On a mile-long assembly line, Ford finally assembled a bomber in one hour instead of the usual several weeks per plane.

In converting farm property to the Willow Run factory, Henry Ford was concerned about the wildlife that would be disturbed by the conversion. He had Ray Dahlinger, his farm manager, and the farm workers trap the animals and move them to a more protected area. Henry Ford's gentleness and concern for nature and the environment impressed me that he continued to be a great naturalist like his old camping buddy, John Burroughs. The public image of harshness never quite reflected the true man.

During this urgent period, Edsel Ford's health problems were becoming more serious, and his father's health also was questionable. As the elder Ford became more withdrawn because of his lack of interest in the war effort, Harry Bennett continued to prevail upon him that Bennett was the most trustworthy man. Bennett made every effort to discredit Sorensen and his capable staff in the aircraft project by telling Mr. Ford that Sorensen was receiving too much public press. Bennett continued to place his men in key production activities, with the idea that he could finally take control of the Ford operations. He established situations whereby he could discredit Edsel's and Sorensen's major support group. Unfortunately, Mr. Ford was misled to the point that Bennett obtained approval to dismiss one by one the loyal group that had built Ford Motor Company, the core group of Edsel's and Sorensen's staff.

As mentioned previously, during World War II Edsel assigned his two sons, Henry Ford II and Benson Ford, to the Product Engineering activity at Gate #4 of the Rouge factory. There the two young men received their first opportunity to work as regular laborers. They were given menial jobs such as assembling experimental car chassis and greasing and lubricating test machines. They wore typical coveralls and carried lunch boxes, similar to the other workers. Both Henry II and Benson fit well into the situation and were not given any special privileges. We were all rather young and enjoyed the camaraderie of our fellow workers.

Henry II and Benson both had matured since their preteen period when they caused much confusion during their visits with the elder Ford to the old Dearborn Engineering Laboratory. In the earlier period, their grandfather loved their visits to Fair Lane, and he would bring his grandsons to the laboratory on weekends and give them free reign of the area. The boys would borrow a car and drive wildly around the facility. They took great delight in taking the rack of time cards and mixing them to frustrate the workers on Monday, particularly those who were late. Being mischievous himself, Mr. Ford accepted this behavior.

Henry II had been married only a short time when he started work at the Product Engineering facility at the Rouge plant. We teased him about what his new bride thought about his greasy appearance when he returned from work. In his good-natured way, he laughed and said she did not think he had a very important job. It was my pleasure to have had the opportunity to tell him that if he worked hard and applied himself, he soon would have a better job.

We all recognized that someday Henry II would be our big boss; however, we enjoyed joking with him about his current situation. He took the kidding in a good-natured way and enjoyed the training experience. I told him about the time when, as a teenager, I asked for more money and his grandfather had responded, "Liking your work was most important, as in doing so you would apply yourself and be successful." Of course, I did not remind Henry II that his grandfather at that time was a billionaire, while I was earning 13 cents per hour.

Henry Ford (right) and his grandson Henry Ford II (left) in 1944.

Henry II was liked by all the staff and worked hard to prove himself. He took very little time off. However, one day he wanted to smoke, and I reminded him that company rules did not permit smoking in the factory. We took an experimental car and drove out of the factory to the gravel road leading from the Rouge factory to Greenfield Village. We parked along the side of the road, which was rather scenic and abundant with trees and the beauty of nature. While leisurely viewing the scene, chatting and puffing clouds of smoke, a car approached, blowing up a screen of dust and headed for the Rouge factory. Unfortunately, Charles Sorensen and Henry Ford, Sr. were in the car. As they passed us, their car slowed and they observed the two of us smoking. This concerned me, and I told Henry II that if Sorensen told Sheldrick I was out smoking, I could be in real trouble. Although Henry II was sympathetic to my concern, he replied by saying that he hoped his grandfather would not feel he was goofing off.

During this early training period of Henry II and Benson, we were developing the prototype of the Jeep and other military projects at Gate #4 of the Rouge factory. At this time, Edsel Ford and Charles Sorensen were actively directing Larry Sheldrick and our small group with little direction from Henry Ford, Sr. Upon completion of the first Jeep prototype and shipment to the Department of Defense in Halobird, Maryland, for approval, we arranged to show the vehicle to Edsel, Sorensen, and a few other management people. We arranged to have the two young Fords drive the vehicle out of a wooded rough area to show its unusual operating characteristics. With much fanfare, the two young Fords burst on the scene with great acceptance and pride from their father and the attendees.

This show was much more receptive than when we tried to demonstrate the amphibian version of the little Jeep. Our first prototype was built at the Rouge factory, and we decided it should be run down into the boat slip that accommodated the 700-foot boats delivering iron ore to the foundry. Thus, we built a ramp down into the boat slip and made the necessary preparations for a similar exciting presentation. Fortunately, the two young Fords were not driving this vehicle. When the vehicle hit the water, it proceeded to sink after traveling only a few feet. Someone had forgotten to install one of the floor panels. We also had not asked the driver to wear a life vest. Fortunately, the driver could swim.

The little Jeep was a remarkable vehicle and seemed to fulfill all the Department of Defense expectations. Upon completion of the durability test at Halobird and approval for production, we wanted to show the military officials how capable the Jeep was. We had tested it in rough cross-country conditions and had successfully traversed the large mud puddle used to test the tanks and tank-retriever vehicles. We arranged with the Hollywood news media to show how well the vehicle could cross the large mud bath. The media positioned a camera on the far side of the mud bath (200 feet across), and our four well-polished young soldiers drove the vehicle at full speed into the mud puddle. Little did we know that during the previous night, larger vehicles had used the puddle and its depth had increased. As the camera commenced and the vehicle hit the pond, the vehicle started to settle and made it halfway to the other side. The handsome young operators sat erect and slowly settled with the vehicle until only their shoulders were above the muddy surface. Being a bit ingenious, we had a tank-retriever winch the vehicle back to shore. We cleaned the Jeep and had the young men restored to normal appearance and started the demonstration again. This time, we had the operators back the Jeep into the pond as far as they dared, without losing traction. Upon a signal, they proudly showed the vehicle emerging from the pond. With clever Hollywood clipping of film, we could show the vehicle going into the pond and successfully coming out. Even with this mishap, we marveled at the capability of the little Jeep to go almost everywhere without difficulty.

One of the unrecognized projects that Edsel Ford agreed to have our group develop was a special reconnaissance vehicle that the British wanted to explore. It was intended to be a mobile machine-gun carrier with a low profile that would permit soldiers to survey the front lines without being too obvious. We designed and produced a small, low-silhouette, flatbed chassis vehicle with four-wheel drive. Large 10×28 inch wheels and tires were used for flotation and traction. The design permitted the machine gunner and helper to lie flat on the platform, thus offering a low silhouette. The driver was positioned at the rear of the vehicle, beside the engine.

The prototype was produced, and Edsel asked Sheldrick to ready it for a show to the British military officials. We drove the vehicle for a final test into an expansive wooded area. It was early springtime, and although the spring thaw had produced many large puddles of water throughout the woods, we ran through them without a problem. As we became more confident, we approached a large black and ominous water hole, and we proceeded with great confidence to go through it at full speed. Unfortunately, the vehicle sank out of sight. We swam to shore and watched the bubbles indicating where we had lost our pride and joy. I went to the nearest phone to tell

The prototype machine gun carrier, in which the British were interested.

Prototype machine-gun carrier with 0.50 caliber gun.

Sheldrick to cancel his appointment with Edsel and his friends. When he asked why, I had to tell him the vehicle had disappeared to the bottom of a swamp. As you can see, working on serious military vehicles has its high and low points.

Upon completion of young Henry II's training at the Rouge plant, he left and enlisted in the military. His father and Sorensen continued directing the engineering development activities with more and more interference from Harry Bennett and his goon squad. Bennett continued to develop a structure of his people throughout the operations to inform him of all detail of operations and the managers' daily operations. He continued to advise Henry Ford, Sr. of situations that would defame loyal and trusted managers of the past. Edsel tried desperately to take sides with Sorensen, Sheldrick, and those he had come to respect. As the key players were fired one by one as a result of Bennett's efforts, Edsel's health deteriorated and our managers became more depressed with the situation. Upon Edsel's death in 1943, the situation seemed hopeless. Bennett seemed to have convinced the elder Ford that Bennett was the only person he could trust.

My boss Sheldrick had become a mentor to Henry II during his early training in 1940 at the Rouge factory. After Edsel's death, Sheldrick attempted to direct Henry II when he was made a vice president in December 1943. Bennett indicated to the elder Mr. Ford that Sheldrick was trying to influence Henry II in the decision-making process without conferring with the senior Ford. Pressure was put on Sheldrick, and he resigned, leaving us without a chief engineer. Bennett continued to undermine Sorensen and John Crawford (Edsel's right-hand man), and both men finally quit.

By March 1944, the Ford organization was under the control of the senior Ford and the power of Bennett to prevail with his selected staff. Mr. Ford promoted the head metallurgist Hud McCarroll to head the Product Engineering activity. Answering to McCarroll was Dale Roeder for commercial vehicles, Emory De Nador for Ford passenger cars, Jack Wharam for Lincoln cars, and I for tractors. The product development situation was somewhat in a holding pattern until September 1945, when Henry Ford II was made president and given control of the company. Fortunately, Clara Ford (wife of Henry Ford, Sr.) and Eleanor Ford (Edsel Ford's widow) pressured the elder Henry Ford to turn over the management of the Ford Motor Company to his grandson.

Edsel Ford should be given credit for volunteering the Ford resources to the war effort and for carrying on corporate management under a distressing situation. A much less sensitive individual might have survived the torment of seeing his loyal team being destroyed by Bennett's misdirection of his father, Henry Ford.

Chapter 11

Postwar Period

During the period between Edsel Ford's death in 1943 and Henry Ford II becoming president of Ford Motor Company in 1945, each of the four Product Engineering groups was somewhat on their own. The total Product Engineering group at this time numbered fewer than 100 people. Military activities had diminished, and the four groups were directing their attention to postwar projects. Decisions were in the hands of the senior Henry Ford. Henry Ford II was spending much of his time in assessing the problems of the various areas and still had no decision-making authority prior to 1945. Because of the limited number of engineering staff, I continued to have responsibility for passenger car transmission and rear axle designs in addition to the tractor engineering activity.

As the four product groups worked on various new postwar designs, Mr. Ford continued to control decision making. Thus, we remained inhibited by his requirement to use the transverse spring suspension system for the car instead of the more comfortable-riding four-spring suspension used by our competitors. With Edsel Ford's encouragement, we had developed other more advanced features, but we had to put them on hold because of his father's insistence for a two-spring suspension.

The passenger car group was working on an updated prewar chassis design which would incorporate a hypoid rear axle to replace the spiral bevel type design. We developed a design and produced samples. Unfortunately, this type of axle was functionally incompatible with the two-spring suspension having a torque tube and radius rods. Start-up vibration from lack of lubricant film strength, necessary for hypoid gearing, created an unacceptable vibration.

With increased tractor design activity, the Ford management permitted me to hire a young engineer named Hans Mathias from Chevrolet to take over the rear axle project, and the production transmission design activity was transferred to others. The hypoid axle finally was adopted when the suspension of the postwar car was changed to four springs and the torque tube between the transmission and rear axle was eliminated.

During World War II and my absence to work on Jeeps and tanks, the Ford tractor group was in a holding pattern. Because of a lack of critical materials during the war, tractor production was reduced substantially. As previously mentioned, an updated Model 2N was developed which conserved critical materials such as rubber and copper. A limited run of these tractors was produced. During this period, Ferguson had increased his small engineering staff to help plan future products. He had hired a chief engineer from the Minne-Moline and John Deere competitive companies.

Upon my return to the tractor program, the Ferguson group was trying to promote a second size of tractor. It was obvious to me the group was being influenced by having hired engineers from the competition to assist in planning. These engineers wanted to perpetuate the typical row-crop high-clearance type of tractors with which they were most familiar. Ferguson suggested that I have my staff prepare sketches of a larger-size tractor incorporating features similar to those of the competition's tractors. This was done, and the tractor was designated the Model 4P. Experimental samples were produced and tested.

By this time, Henry Ford II was taking an active part in decision making because of his grandfather's health problems. Henry II was not as concerned with the desires of Ferguson as was his grandfather, who had made the verbal agreement with Ferguson. Upon our review of the new project with Henry Ford II, he told Ferguson that if Ford lost as much money on a second design as they had up to the present period, he did not think the project could be justified. Ultimately, the project was cancelled.

Relations had never been good between Ford management and Ferguson. Somewhat similar to Bennett's tactics, Ferguson had used the elder Henry Ford as a shield against Ford management when Ford Motor Conpany wanted to increase the tractor price. As mentioned previously, the 1939 Ford tractor was priced to Ferguson without a true cost analysis. The tractor was produced in the Rouge factory, along with the passenger car. Actual costs for producing the tractor were unknown; the passenger car carried much of the

Experimental prototype of the Model 4P tractor, 1945.

overhead. Ferguson also occupied free space at the Rouge factory for his administrative activities for a period of time. Finally, the tractor manufacturing was separated from the car production area and moved to the Highland Park factory, where the old Model T car had been produced. With the move, more accurate costs were determined, and Sorensen pressured Ferguson to increase the price of the vehicle. Ferguson would tell Sorensen to speak to Mr. Ford about Sorensen's lack of ability to produce the tractor at a lower cost. Obviously, he knew Sorensen would not admit to such a problem.

After Ferguson–Sherman established a distribution system by taking over Eber Sherman's national Fordson organization, Ferguson finally forced Sherman out of the activity. It was Sherman who had brought Ferguson to Mr. Ford's attention. As time passed and the N series of tractors became more popular, Ferguson grew more confident of being able to go on his own. He told me many times that he thought his name on the tractor should be more prominent than the Ford name. It was necessary to remind Ferguson that Mr. Ford's reputation was the reason the tractor was successful and that he should be grateful for all that Mr. Ford had contributed to his success. By this time, Ferguson had forgotten about his failure with David Brown.

In working with Ferguson, it became obvious to me that he was quite a schemer. His past activities indicated his cleverness in accomplishing his objectives. When Ferguson would not agree to increase the price of the tractor so it might be profitable to Ford, he suggested to Sorensen before he quit Ford in 1944 that he would have an industrial consulting service review Ford manufacturing operations. By so doing, the consulting service could suggest more efficient ways of manufacturing, resulting in lower production costs. Until this period, Ferguson did not have access to the drawings and manufacturing processes used to produce the tractor because Ferguson's group was a marketing operation. Upon Sorensen's agreement to permit Ferguson to provide the study for cost reduction, we were asked to provide detailed drawings and all proprietary information necessary to produce the tractor. With this information in Ferguson's hands, his group started to solicit some of Ford's major suppliers such as Bendix, which provided car brakes. Ferguson's group wanted these suppliers to provide quotes as a supplier to Ferguson of tractor components. Other Ford suppliers informed the Ford management that Ferguson was using Ford drawings for quotes. This subterfuge by the Ferguson organization became evident. Unfortunately for Ferguson, it involved Ernest Breech, chairman of the board of Bendix, who in 1946 was hired by Henry Ford II to help reorganize the Ford Motor Company.

When Breech became settled at Ford Motor Company, he discovered that Ford had lost money in supplying tractors to Ferguson but that Ferguson had done extremely well. Breech suggested to Ferguson that the profits should be in proportion to the assets invested. Ferguson had only a small staff with typical office equipment and was not impressed with the offer from Breech. As negotiations continued without agreement, Breech then advised Ferguson that as of a certain date, Ford would not be a supplier to Ferguson.

Ford management proceeded to set up an independent tractor distribution system called Dearborn Motors. The limited investment to perform the previous Ferguson operations was provided by a few Ford executives.

With the advent of Dearborn Motors, my tractor group was asked to develop a new tractor based on the original Model 9N but with the addition of many new features. Thus, we developed the Model 8N with many improvements in steering, operator station, hydraulics, and other features. To identify the tractor as a new model, I suggested we select a new color scheme. The typical gunmetal gray of that period, which was used on machine tools and battleships, was not the best considering that as the paint thinned from age, rust would show through the paint. Competitors such as International Harvester were using red paint to overcome this deficiency. Because paint color identified various makes of tractors, I suggested we use a two-tone paint job. The management was asked to pick their two favorite colors for consideration. As expected, the management usually picked their own school colors. At the time, my wife Judy had an attractive dress that was a combination of red and silver gray. I envisioned that the red chassis would not show rust with age and the silver-gray sheet metal would not show distress from chickens roosting on the tractor and discoloration from other contaminants around the barnyard. It was my responsibility to tabulate the votes on color scheme, and I was pleased that my color suggestion was selected. With all of the structured organization of today, this simple process would be doomed to failure.

Upon introduction of the Model 8N Ford tractor in 1947, the Ferguson tractor dealers abandoned Ferguson and joined the Dearborn Motors distribution system. As previously mentioned, most of these dealers were Fordson tractor dealers of the past; therefore, they were returning home, so to speak. Because Ferguson lost a major portion of his distribution system and his supplier, he decided to sue Ford for $251 million, for conspiracy to put him out of business. A lesser amount of $11 million was for infringement of patents Ferguson held in his name. This is quite an interesting exercise because it was Ferguson who started the ruckus in obtaining Ford proprietary information for his undercover purposes. Furthermore, Ferguson had asked Henry Ford to allow him to take out the tractor patents in his name, despite the fact that Ferguson was not the inventor.

This lawsuit resulted in multimillion-dollar legal costs by both parties in trying to reach a settlement. Several years of depositions and thousands of hours of patent search for prior art resulted in many key participants dying or losing their memories (perhaps by convenience). For instance, Ferguson's deposition indicated he could remember things only during certain periods of the year, and he was not too certain when those periods would occur. The courts

The prototype of the Model 8N tractor, which had a color scheme of red and silver-gray.

finally decided the suit should be settled and both parties should get on with their businesses. This was a relief to Ford management, and a settlement was made in favor of Ferguson for $9 million, most of which had to be used for his legal expenses. This was much less than the multimillions Ferguson had requested. The patents were never litigated to prove their validity, which was fortunate for both parties because it prevented competition from using these unique designs until the patents expired.

At a later date, Ferguson finally went into production in England, using the drawings and processes obtained from Ford to produce the Model 9N tractor. This model was called "TE-20." Ford brought out the Model 8N tractor. As previously stated, this was the original classic design, but it was enhanced by many new features and its new identification of a red and silver-gray color scheme. Fortunately, 1947 provided an excellent market for new farm equipment and a fresh marketing approach. In the preceding seven years, farmers had become familiar with the appeal of the tractor with the three-point hitch

The Model TE-20 Ferguson tractor, copied from the Ford Model 9N tractor. (Randy Leffingwell, shown in his book Ford Farm Tractors.*)*

attachment versus that of the competition. The popularity of the Model 8N resulted in a level of production constituting 25 percent of the total U.S. tractor production. This is remarkable because the major manufacturers such as International Harvester, John Deere, Case, Allis-Chalmers, Oliver, and others were producing many different tractor models and sizes, whereas Ford offered only the one tractor of unique design with no options, somewhat similar to the Model T car with no paint options. Production continued at a rate of 100,000 per year, and the Ford tractors continued to be shipped 14 to a boxcar. I have been told that after 50 years of history, approximately 750,000 of this series of tractors remain in use today, and they sell for a price of five times more than what they sold for when new. Worldwide production of the basic design now numbers in the millions, because Ferguson produced the copy in England and licensed others to produce the same design. It was interesting to see recently that the many retreating Kosovo population used tractors of this design to transport their families from the war zone.

The record now shows that my mentor, Henry Ford, Sr., accomplished his dream of providing farmers with a product that would do for farmers what the Model T did for transportation. As mentioned previously, all tractors world-wide that are produced today have copied the classic design of chassis and implement controls of the 1939 Ford model. The consumer has benefited substantially by the interchangeability resulting from a standardized uniform implement hitch. No longer does a farmer have to purchase new implements when changing to another brand of tractor.

With the transfer of management authority to Henry Ford II, the Ford management team concentrated its attention on restructuring the corporation to be competitive with General Motors and Chrysler. Tractor activities continued with little attention from those involved in the car interests. The tractor operations were in a leadership position within the industry without the need of a large, cumbersome, and costly organizational structure typical of the automotive industry.

Chapter 12

Ford Reorganization

When he became president of Ford Motor Company in 1945, Henry Ford II was faced with the task of developing a new management organizational structure and creating a completely new corporate image. Because of Harry Bennett's inroads in placing his men in key positions, Henry II felt uncomfortable about promoting from within the company. Thus, Henry II's first step was a wise one—he fired Bennett and as many of Bennett's key players as could be identified. Unfortunately, many of the managers that had built the company under the elder Henry Ford and Edsel Ford were no longer available to young Henry. He rather quickly recognized that he needed to build a team of loyal players with proven experience. Henry II was fortunate to have found a key player in John Bugas, who had been an F.B.I. agent in Detroit. Bugas had been hired by Edsel Ford to determine where company materials were disappearing, and he was assigned to Harry Bennett as an assistant. With factory security under Bennett, factory materials were disappearing. Bugas was familiar with Bennett and his operations. His first task was to fire his boss and in turn identify those Henry II could trust and those Henry II should fire.

With no organizational structure, Henry II began recruiting help. He was fortunate in obtaining a group of ten brilliant U.S. Air Force officers who had been responsible for planning strategic Air Force activities. The complexities of planning and controlling such a major operation were recognized as the type of help needed to develop a strategic action plan for the recovery of Ford Motor Company. When these ten brilliant and enthusiastic young men arrived on the scene at Ford, they knew little about operations of the company.

With their notebooks in hand and by asking unlimited questions, they identified the major problems and challenges. These men took so much of our time that initially we called them the "Quiz Kids." As they finally settled into the

121

A 1953 photograph of Henry Ford II.

company and identified many basic problems at Ford, they promoted themselves to being known as the "Whiz Kids." While these ten young recruits were picking the brains of the various operations, Henry II recognized that he needed a key experienced and proven executive to help him embrace the many problems within the company.

Ernest Kanzler, Henry II's uncle, had been a consultant to Edsel Ford in Edsel's early career. He had considerable influence on Edsel's efforts to bring better organization to the company and was mistrusted by the elder Ford as trying to mislead Edsel. Kanzler finally separated from the company, but he was recognized by the Ford family as a shrewd judge of business leaders. He was a successful businessman and held a seat on the Bendix board of directors.

In 1946, Ernest Breech was chairman of the board of Bendix. As mentioned previously, Bendix was a supplier of brakes for the Ford Motor Company.

Bendix was one of the companies that Ferguson had approached to provide quotes on the Ford tractor designs. Henry II had met Breech several times and was impressed by him. Breech had 23 years of experience with General Motors before joining Bendix. His broad experience made him a candidate for heading a major corporation such as Ford Motor Company.

When Breech was offered the challenge to help reorganize Ford Motor Company, he wisely recognized he would need proven experience to assist him. He contacted several of his General Motors associates to determine if they would join him if he went to Ford. They agreed, and Breech joined Ford Motor Company in May 1946. He came with a team of associates experienced in product engineering, finance, manufacturing, and legal matters.

Tex Thornton, who headed the ten Whiz Kids, had made a bid for the top job prior to Breech being hired. When Breech arrived at Ford Motor Company, he had Thornton and the Whiz Kids report to his new team member Lewis Crusoe. Crusoe fired Thornton and assigned his group to various functions as part of his restructuring and assigning functional responsibilities.

Crusoe also was a proven General Motors Fisher Body executive. He finally was given responsibility for the new Ford Division of the corporation. This was a move toward decentralization, similar to the organizational structure of General Motors.

With the Ford Motor Company reorganization, Henry II and Breech took giant steps to reinspire a depressed organization and regenerate the enthusiasm of the staff. With the charisma of the two leaders, a breath of fresh air seemed to permeate all areas of the Ford empire. No longer were employees abused by Harry Bennett and his goon squad. Fortunately, young Henry II had been part of our factory operations as a young trainee and had learned firsthand what conspiracy was taking place to mislead his grandfather. He was familiar with Bennett's hold on his grandfather and knew firsthand from his parents how this situation resulted in his father's early and untimely death from frustration.

Young Henry II quickly demonstrated that he was a good listener and that he recognized his need to be trained by his proven executives. With his experience in the U.S. Navy and his travels throughout the Ford factory, he realized the importance of rebuilding the morale of the organization. Henry II started a new program of human engineering to empower and dignify his employees and to show respect for their efforts. For Henry II's troops, this was similar to Moses leading the Israelites out of bondage. It put new life and vigor into the old-timers who had remained at Ford Motor Company and were waiting for a better day.

Ernest Breech had great strength and experience as an organization man. As previously stated, Breech had been an executive with General Motors prior to becoming chairman of the board of Bendix. His experience and advice were real assets to young Henry II in restructuring all operations of the corporation. The small Product Engineering activity was revitalized by Breech, bringing in William James from Studebaker Corporation and Harold Youngren from Borg-Warner Corporation. These two executives began recruiting engineers from all other automotive competitors. Hud McCarroll, the key metallurgist and interim engineering head who replaced Larry Sheldrick at Ford Motor Company, was replaced by proven product engineering executives. They quickly recognized that our small group of 200 no longer was adequate to keep Ford products competitive. With the authority to reorganize, engineering grew by leaps and bounds, and the long-overdue and necessary development resources were added.

Talent was hired from all other competitive car manufacturers. At first, this resulted in some confusion and a real mishmash of planning because each engineer came to the table with the postwar plans of his parent company. However, this all was resolved with good planning and empowerment of the various staffs. However, because of timing, the postwar 1946 Ford car did not differ substantially from the prewar model. With input from the many new product engineers and manufacturers, the 1949 Ford car reflected the talents of both the old-timers and the new recruits. Finally, the suspension of the car was changed to four springs, and major car body appointments were offered, similar to those offered by competitors.

Edsel Ford's long-overdue vision of restructuring Ford Motor Company into a more effective operation finally was occurring. It was obvious to us that Henry II was trying desperately to accomplish what his father was never permitted to achieve.

The engineering management of Ford Motor Company in 1946.

Business procedures and practices that had never been important to the senior Ford now became critical objectives of the new management. Because this effort required an enormous amount of paperwork and the major new management group was concerned with more important matters, the Whiz Kids accumulated much data for presentation and approval by senior management. Because of the great exposure these young Whiz Kids received, they progressed rapidly in the organization and became a powerful group in the decision-making process. Their academic training permitted them to outdebate the old-timers and in most cases convince the new management they were the source of great wisdom.

Detailed operating procedures were long overdue; however, as would be expected, many of the practices were too bureaucratic in concept. The pendulum was swinging from no paperwork to more than ample. I am certain that the major management, having been trained in the ways of General Motors, followed their own bias in remaking Ford into a similar control process. Although I have great respect for finance staff and their functions, they seem to generate more paperwork than necessary to produce a product. Although the elder Henry Ford was too restrictive with recordkeeping, it became obvious to many of us that young Henry Ford II was being led "down the primrose path" to over-organization as it applied to cost controls. However, after the good work of establishing new operating procedures and employees relations, every effort was made to achieve control of costs.

Prior to reorganization, Ford Motor Company functioned as a centralized type of organization. This resulted from the senior Henry Ford not having an organizational chart containing many layers of supervision that resulted in subsequent building of bureaucracies. Henry Ford believed that more money might be spent on determining detail costs than would be saved. Furthermore, it would have inhibited his style of making rapid decisions.

As the finance-trained managers became more empowered in the decision-making process, efforts were made to determine more exact costs. Henry Ford II finally was convinced to decentralize the operations into typical cost centers, which was the same practice followed by General Motors. This was typical of the day and promised fulfillment of those who liked to play with numbers (often referred to as "bean counters" by those they tried to control).

This effort resulted in quadrupling the Product Engineering staff. The group had expanded substantially before this process was put into effect. With a centralized product engineering activity, products within the engineering group were assigned to those who had special skills. For instance, all engine development was placed under one group. Body engineering was placed under another group, and transmissions and axles were placed under another group. The end-product vehicles, such as Ford, Mercury, Lincoln, and trucks, were established as divisions of the corporation. Previously, when the yearly engineering budget was developed, each group estimated its costs to be charged to the various divisions. This resulted in the divisional heads not having control of the detailed engineering costs. As would be expected, with decentralization the divisions wanted complete control of costs; therefore, the engine engineers were assigned to the Engine and Foundry Manufacturing Division, the car body engineering engineers were assigned to the Sheet Metal Division, and so forth. Unfortunately, inasmuch as birds of a feather seem to flock together, the finance-trained personnel were put in charge of most of the manufacturing divisions.

When staffing of the various engineering groups of each of these divisions was executed, it resulted in tremendous growth within the engineering activity. For instance, when the chief engineer of the Ford Division was charged with dealing with his Ford engine supplier or a purchased engine, he then became required to specify and qualify the product for acceptance. He asked for his share of the engineers previously being charged to the Ford Division as a centralized operation. He was told that the engineers were specialized—for instance, a crankshaft expert, cylinder block expert, etc. Therefore, they could not supply one for each of the new end-product divisions. This resulted in each division duplicating the skills and hiring its own engineers. This also was typical when the divisions tried to separate other resources. Ultimately, the effort to establish profit centers resulted in a tremendous need for additional workers, resulting to a great extent in duplication of effort.

This explanation is not intended to cast a shadow on good cost control; rather, it only indicates that too many "bean counters" flocking together can be counterproductive. The greatest negative to over-control is that it inhibits the process of development because of the long time constraints of processing paperwork. This is discouraging and dampens the enthusiasm of the innovators of new ideas.

I have always felt that the process of Henry Ford Sr. coming to the Product Engineering Department in the morning with an idea and saying in his enthusiastic way, " I will be back this afternoon to see how the idea is working out" was a more effective means of operation. Obviously, as organizations grow and projects multiply, limited controls must be developed to set priorities. However, large corporations now are recognizing the need to establish project teams, composed of all the necessary disciplines for decision making, and empowering those teams to make the decisions and proceed with the project. This is proving effective today in bringing products to market with reduced turnaround time. More importantly, the products more closely meet the objectives because of the ownership by a team responsible for the project outcome.

Successful organizations of today no longer find it acceptable to have isolated bureaucracies of special skills that perform their operations and then throw the project over the fence for the next group to pick up its functions. More importantly, the development of human skills is enhanced by exposing various talents to situations that stretch their capabilities. As with every successful entrepreneur, who starts with a few workers needing many skills, each employee learns from the others. Clerks and sweepers soon recognize that, with additional training and special formal education courses, they can progress upward in an organization.

A good example occurred in the early days of Ford Motor Company and the Model T car. The senior Henry Ford had a sweeper named John Wandersee, who became interested in foundry practice. With experience and some additional study, John became the head metallurgist at Ford Motor Company. During the infancy days of the auto industry, the art of making good metal was similar to baking bread on a stove fired by corncobs. John Wandersee developed unusual skills in mixing additives to a melt of metal and knowing exactly when to tap the melt. I was fortunate to have John's help during my training period in the foundry.

I have observed that as organizations grow, functional organizational structures are developed to control work output rather than to determine the best way to develop a better product and the skills of the work force. This usually results in little kingdoms being formed, which are guarded carefully from outside influence. This frequently smothers talent that is restricted by doing repetitive work, and it offers limited personal growth to individuals.

The elder Henry Ford taught me early in my career that I could follow his example and try to offer each employee I meet an opportunity for growth. For example, I observed that typing pools never seemed busy and the workers there certainly were not excited about their jobs. In response to my observation, my boss at that time permitted me to assign many of the typists to project teams. When those typists completed the project of limited typing, they were assigned to help the engineers in their development activities. The typists soon realized that they needed formal training in reading blueprints. After mastering this skill, they often would attend night school to obtain sufficient education to advance. In numerous cases, the typists advanced to the status of engineer. One of my young typists, John Damian, finally became a successful attorney, and many of my young clerks developed engineering skills. This was true with other workers in skilled trades. Too often, individuals are locked into groups that offer little opportunity for developing their inherent talents. Fortunately, Henry Ford II recognized the advantage of encouraging educational programs for employees, and he established financial support to encourage them in their careers.

Henry Ford II certainly listened to new ideas and supported them in most cases with good judgment. However, some of his staff had their own "axes to grind," and they made efforts to mislead young Henry II. As with all major corporations, infighting for positions prevails at times, thus making it difficult for the top executive to know whom to trust. Henry Ford II was blessed with the same sincere, straightforward honesty of his father Edsel and, to a certain extent, the determination of his grandfather to be a strong decision maker. Henry II also exemplified the same characteristics as his father Edsel in being courteous and a good listener. Henry II was wise in having successful executives to help train him in good decision-making skills. He recognized that his father was not permitted to delegate and empower others to accomplish his particular agenda; therefore, Henry II made every effort to conquer these shortcomings.

It was rather obvious that the driving spirit behind Henry II was one of accomplishing what his father Edsel was inhibited from doing. Young Henry II worked hard and long hours to fulfill the many obligations he felt important to the job at hand. The challenge was important, and he did not want to turn it over to others. Although he listened to the advice of his management team, Henry II took a more active role in making decisions.

Henry II was a good student. As he became more confident in his judgment, he became more aggressive, similar to his grandfather. With tutoring from Ernest Breech, Henry II gained confidence in his inherent ability to be a leader. His changing of major management several times indicated that he wanted to be the decision maker rather than a follower. For a while, we expected young Henry II to be as fearful as his grandfather was in determining whom he could trust. With indecision, Henry II went outside the Ford corporation and hired Bunky Knudsen from General Motors to head the operation. The infighters soon discredited Knudsen in the eyes of Henry II, and Knudsen was fired. Continuing management changes occurred until Lee Iacocca finally reached the top position in the Ford organization.

Henry Ford II (left) and Ernest Breech (right) in 1946.

Unfortunately, Henry II became more involved with outside civic and overseas travel, which permitted Iacocca to become the major decision maker in Henry II's absence. Henry II eventually believed that Iacocca was becoming so important that Iacocca was attracting more attention than Henry II was. This is when Henry II informed Iacocca that he no longer liked him, which must have been very discouraging to Iacocca. However, time has proven that the change was good for both Ford and Chrysler. It was evident to many Ford managers that Iacocca had such confidence in his decision-making ability that he felt he could "walk on water." At this time, Chrysler was headed by two finance executives, which is the worst of all combinations because the numbers game can predict only how soon one will be going out of business. These two executives could not decide the future of the corporation. Iacocca was the right man for envisioning how the Chrysler organization could continue.

During the reorganization of Ford Motor Company by Henry II and the Whiz Kids, a corporate Product Planning Department was established to assist the Product Engineering activity in its future design concepts. In most cases, this group monitored competition and, to some extent, directed the engineers' design concepts. These groups strongly influenced the decisions made by top management, and their observations about competitive market trends greatly influenced product projections. Obviously, the groups would examine what was on the market and prevail upon engineering to provide similar designs. Instead of being visionaries, a "me too" attitude too often resulted in untimeliness and poor market acceptance. For instance, when Chevrolet sales finally exceeded those of Ford, the Ford planning and marketing group concluded that Ford should offer a six-cylinder option to the V8 to increase popularity. No sooner did Ford offer the option than Chevrolet developed a V8. The major part of the auto industry then moved to the V8 concept that had prevailed at Ford since its popular introduction in 1932.

The disastrous Edsel car also was such a program. The planning activity prevailed upon Henry Ford II that a car between the Ford and the Mercury and between the Mercury and the Lincoln would assure that Ford would not lose market to the midsize cars of its competition. With smaller steps between products, customers would not be tempted to cross over to other product lines. For instance, a Ford owner who could not afford to upgrade to a Mercury would purchase a Pontiac or Dodge and thus might not be a future Ford owner.

Henry II questioned the wisdom of the Edsel car project; however, with the Product Planning Department supported by Ernest Breech, the project was pursued. The market timing was unsuccessful because of the great proliferation of models offered by competition, in combination with a weak market. The unfortunate Edsel car program was doomed to failure.

As the corporate program planning committees grew in size, they convinced Henry Ford II that the Tractor Division also should have such a group to assist in forward planning. As you might expect, several key tractor engineers were hired from competitors to help my group plan its future tractor designs. At the time, we had 25 percent of the total market with one model of tractor instead of many models offered by the competition. Likewise, we were in an enviable position with respect to the rest of the industry. All this success had been accomplished without outside help.

The new recruits arrived and prevailed upon management that if we would design tractors similar to those of our competitors, we would add to our market share. I asked these recruits to demonstrate to me how the large tricycle tractors with front cultivators could outperform the Ford tractor. In field demonstrations, we could prove that the little Ford tractor could go into the field and finish cultivating before the operators of competitive tractors could round up all attachments necessary to begin. This was not convincing to the group, and they prevailed upon management also to furnish these types of tractors. With great reluctance, we were pressured to follow the supervisor's directive and to develop these new products. The end result was that Ford's market share did not change. Furthermore, because of the multiple models, the tractors could no longer be shipped 14 in a boxcar. Costs increased, while manufacturing and dealer investments increased and volume decreased. A few years later, the rest of industry changed its designs to copy the original Ford concept. By this time, Ford had lost its important advantage of low cost, which had been a major objective of the senior Henry Ford.

It is obvious that strategic planning is an important function of successful organizations; however, the structure of committees must weigh heavily toward those directly involved with consumer concerns. In the farm equipment industry, the development staff work on a daily basis with users to develop products that meet users' future requirements instead of merely monitoring the competition.

The reorganization of Ford Motor Company was directed primarily toward the car divisions, whereas the Tractor Division finally was requested to follow a similar organizational structure. My early training and experience with the senior Henry Ford did not effectively equip me to work within such a bureaucratic structure. I remained with Ford until 1959, when I found myself involved in a situation that I did not like. As frequently happens in all organizations, several factions were sparring for position within Ford Motor Company.

One of these groups wanted to dispose of me to put a product into production that I indicated was doomed to failure. I resigned from Ford Motor Company after serving there for 30 years, and I joined John Deere and Co. to help redesign its products to more modern concepts. This appealed to me because it again offered me an opportunity to innovate and to work in a one-on-one management style that I believed was conducive to making real progress.

Since my departure from Ford Motor Company, my predecessors put the questionable product into production and later were fired from Ford when the factory was closed to try to correct this major program mistake. I hasten to mention that my separation from Ford Motor Company occurred while Henry Ford II was out of the country and the traducers could prevail upon those less concerned and knowledgeable to permit them to act. My move to John Deere has kept me abreast of farm equipment worldwide. With great nostalgia, I have watched as the farm equipment industry continues to shrink in numbers. This consolidation has resulted in the Ford Motor Company no longer offering a farm tractor and John Deere being among the few surviving farm equipment companies. With the death of the senior Henry Ford, it was inevitable that more excitement and interest would be directed toward Ford's car business.

Since leaving Ford Motor Company in 1959, I have observed with great interest the many organizational changes of Ford management. It is obvious to me that each of the many management changes had its own strengths and weaknesses. It is most commendable that Henry II finally built a potential management team that permitted promoting from within the organization. Furthermore, he broadened the disciplines of top management to achieve improved balance. When I left the company, it was dominated by financial management with controls that stifled progress. It becomes obvious to an outsider that Ford now has overcome much of its early power struggles from within. The market reflects the fine progress Ford has made in building sound management and good labor relations. The recovery of Ford Motor Company reflects Henry Ford II's dedication to the employees and public by restoring Ford Motor Company to its former position of importance within the industry.

Henry Ford II has set a high standard for future generations of his family in his dedication beyond self-interest to further the mission of Ford Motor Company. The archives are filled with examples of second and third generations of companies squandering the fortunes of the successful first generation. Through his persistent dedication to save the Ford Motor Company, Henry Ford II had precious little time for other interests. The welfare of the company came first.

Henry Ford II's tireless efforts to expand Ford's global market, as well as his many dedicated efforts to improve the city of Detroit, are a matter of record. He followed in his father's footsteps in taking a leadership role in rebuilding distressed downtown areas of Detroit. Edsel Ford also had been a major player in civic activities that included large investments in the Detroit Arts Institute.

Henry Ford II's many time-consuming activities are noteworthy, because he could have walked away from the challenge and had time to pursue many other interests. Having dedicated himself to the welfare of the company, its workers, and consumers, Henry Ford II recognized the challenge of those who would follow in his footsteps. During my last visit with Henry II, he expressed his concern about his son Edsel II following in his footsteps. Prior to our meeting, I had met the young Edsel II at a Junior Achievement "Hall of Fame" awards banquet where he was accepting an award for his great-grandfather Henry Ford. At this banquet, I had the pleasure of visiting with Edsel II, and I inquired about his future with the Ford Motor Company. Edsel II indicated his desire to continue his service with the company and perhaps step into the shoes of his father at a future date. At a later meeting in Detroit, I had the pleasure of visiting with Henry Ford II, and I expressed my delight in finding a young man who aspired to replace him. When I told Henry II that this young man was his son Edsel II, Henry II's reply was, "Why would he want the job? It is a tough, demanding, and time-consuming job." This comment gave me the impression that the position was so demanding that Henry II questioned the ability of a family member to face the time constraints and demands of the job as he had done. I hope the younger Fords will continue to pursue and build on the successes of the three Ford men who have done so much for the betterment of mankind.

Epilogue

I would like to conclude this little trip down memory lane by sharing a few personal observations relating to both the past and the future of our industry. Having been an active industry participant during 70 percent of the exciting 1900s, I have learned much from my mentors and coworkers. Fortunately, my current participation on the Hawkeye Community College and Junior Achievement Boards challenges me in offering guidance and opportunities to our young leaders of the future. It also challenges and energizes me to be part of the contagious enthusiasm of young people. I well remember the delight Mr. Ford took in visiting the country schoolhouse in Greenfield Village as he watched the children dancing and skipping. Their twinkling eyes and unruly hair must have reminded Mr. Ford of his early school days.

My mentor was a great visionary with a primary objective of furthering the welfare of the people. With his financial success, Henry Ford, Sr. was little concerned about the profitability of his favorite projects. His greatest successes occurred by production of a unique car and farm tractor. These products were offered to the consumer at a minimum cost that was significantly below that of the competition. It is noteworthy that Henry Ford was thrifty in his personal habits but generous in paying good wages for a fair day's work.

Henry Ford enjoyed being a project manager and had an obsession for micromanaging. His organization outgrew his capability of monitoring details to his satisfaction. This permitted Harry Bennett and his espionage system to gain a strong hold over Ford management and to threaten the future of the company. Henry Ford was typical of many entrepreneurs—they usually are not good business managers.

Edsel Ford and Henry Ford II both displayed great leadership characteristics. Edsel recognized the need for reorganization to keep the corporation an efficient and effective competitor; however, his admiration of his father did not permit Edsel to be his own person. He was a good team builder, offering great promise of shared management style. His great sensitivity, gentleness, and consideration of others caused his father to be concerned that others would easily lead Edsel in the decision-making process.

As Mr. Ford aged, Edsel and his few managers had great difficulty in obtaining concurrence on major management decisions. As Mr. Ford became more withdrawn and spent more time with Harry Bennett, Edsel's loyal followers were replaced by Bennett's appointees. Fortunately, Henry Ford II and other Ford family members forced the senior Henry Ford to withdraw from active management of the company. Young Henry II recognized Bennett's conspiracy to take control of the company. Thus, he fired Bennett and his management team, and he took effective action to return the company to sound footing.

Henry Ford II could have walked away from the situation and lived his own lifestyle; however, he should be admired for his concern in keeping the corporation a viable competitor in the industry. Henry II accepted the challenge of accomplishing what his father Edsel tried so desperately to put into effect. He accomplished this through applying all his energies and talents to the job, leaving him limited time to pursue other options. As was true with his grandfather, the organizational growth finally exceeded Henry II's capability to make sound judgments about whom to believe. As a result, Henry II's management style became more aggressive. He finally built an in-house proven management and was wise enough to choose leaders representing the various disciplines, instead of allowing major control by those having financial backgrounds.

As I look toward the future, I would like to offer a few observations and suggestions to those who continue to work in the automotive industry.

Obviously, the industry has made major strides in recognizing the importance of serving customers by better communication and production of more reliable products. This has been accomplished by developing and utilizing the potential talents of the total work force. It is now recognized that worker development is as important as product development. The empowering of employees, even at the lowest levels, to contribute to the decision-making process has proven effective in assuring product quality and in building teamwork.

Project teams, in place of large bureaucratic-type organizational structures, have proven more effective in meeting shorter time constraints and assuring that project objectives are met. An added advantage is the cross training of disciplines through association and sharing of talents. Furthermore, those having lesser skills are encouraged to obtain additional formal training for advancement. This is particularly important in this rapidly changing period of technology obsolescence.

Creativity of projects should not be smothered with the over-cautious characteristics of finance and legal talent. Too often, we create over-control and kill initiative.

The category of labor and management finally should be abolished, and we should become a nation of workers. Less management, replaced by one-on-one contact, will eliminate much of the misunderstanding brought about by a third party generating mistrust. It is well recognized that unions have played an important part in furthering the interests of workers and should be encouraged within a major operation. However, with global availability of product and the mobility of the work force, it now becomes evident that large international unions serve only a limited function.

It has been my pleasant experience in working with the Japanese to find they are forced to follow a more one-on-one style of communication. This has occurred because it is difficult to type Japanese, and the one-on-one communication style reduces paperwork. Observing their decision-making process reminds me of the process used by the elder Henry Ford, in which time was limited for committee meetings and paper shuffling. Mr. Ford's favorite expression was, "You don't build cars with paper." With reduced organizational structures, wage levels between production workers and top management can be kept within more justifiable levels. It is a well-known fact that people who are led by example, rather than being managed by remote control, work more efficiently and develop a much stronger organizational structure.

The educational system is overdue in encouraging young people to pursue opportunities in science and the skilled trades. We cannot become a nation of information and entertainment with less importance on producing products. The Society of Automotive Engineers (SAE) has a program called "A World In Motion," which is an excellent tool for encouraging young people to pursue the world of science.

More emphasis should be placed on vocational education to reduce high-school and post-high-school dropout rates. Young people need better counseling and guidance about the advantages of increased education. Training at an early age should be directed more toward a marketable vocation. Partnering between industry, high schools, and community colleges should be encouraged to permit hands-on experience and specialized instruction to meet the future needs of industry. This would reduce the dropout rate of students and provide important guidance in helping them achieve their future careers objectives.

It is unfortunate that most four-year graduates of universities go to work in a field unrelated to their education. Many graduates are returning to community colleges to take vocational training that is marketable. Because technology is changing so rapidly, major changes in the delivery of education must take place to meet the special needs of the job market. Fortunately, greater emphasis now is being placed by educational boards and faculties to take advantage of the new advances in delivering education and training. With computers, distance learning capability, and excellent cooperation between business and industry, great strides are being made to address the future needs of the labor market.

With distance learning capability through fiber optics, we should make available formal training around the clock. This is most important for those who are locked into work schedules or have physical or financial restrictions that are not conducive to furthering their education.

Most of us recognize we are blessed as a nation because of our great diversity of talents and our mix of many nationalities. Furthermore, we now have the advantage of instant communication throughout the globe. This creates improved understanding of what we are all about as a nation. Every effort must be made to take advantage of our great resources, both natural and manmade, to enhance our world leadership role. Because of the diversity of our nation, we should work toward providing educational opportunities for all. Each person is precious and, with proper training, offers the promise of contributing to the welfare of all.

I am extremely pleased to have had this opportunity to share my experiences and observations with you. I hope you have enjoyed my reflections about the three Fords, as seen by one who was privileged to have worked with them. They were a remarkable trio and gave of themselves, beyond the call of duty, to further the welfare of others.

Index

About the Author

Harold Brock has more than 50 years of experience in the automotive and tractor industry. He joined Ford Motor Company in 1929, and beginning in 1939 served as chief engineer of tractor engineering for almost 20 years. During these years in which the Ford Motor Company matured, Mr. Brock was privileged to have Henry Ford as his mentor, and he worked with both Edsel Ford and Henry Ford II as well.

In 1959, Mr. Brock left Ford Motor Company to work in the Product Engineering area of John Deere Waterloo Works in Iowa. There he served first as director of product engineering and later as a consultant. From 1980 to 1985, Mr. Brock was on the Joint Venture Board and an engineering consultant for the John Deere and Yanmar Diesel Engine Company.

Mr. Brock has been a member of the Society of Automotive Engineers (SAE) since 1944 and was the SAE president in 1971. He was a founding member of the SAE Mississippi Valley Section and now is an SAE Fellow. In addition, Mr. Brock has been a member of the American Society of Agricultural Engineers since 1950 and is a Fellow member there.

Mr. Brock is a founding board member and a current chairman of the board of the Hawkeye Community College. He also served as chairman of the board from 1965 to 1980. He is both a founding and current board member of Junior Achievement—Blackhawkland, serving as chairman of the board from 1979 to 1980 and again from 1991 to 1992. In addition, Mr. Brock is on the board of the Grout Museum and the Amera-Farm-U.S.A., Inc.